AN ESSEX PIE

" This country is a part of the real England "

AN
ESSEX PIE

opened by

T. M. HOPE

" I put in my thumb and pulled out a plum "

Wood engravings by

JOHN O'CONNOR

COLCHESTER : BENHAM & COMPANY

1951

First published 1951

2009

Composed in Bembo type and printed by
Benham and Company Limited, Colchester

CONTENTS

ACKNOWLEDGMENTS

Dr. R. Vaughan Williams kindly answered my enquiries about the song Bushes and Briars and my thanks are due to him for this, and also to the following for permission to quote from books written by them or of which they hold the copyright.

Miss Friedlaender, for her poem " Name's Sake "
Mrs. Thomas: three poems by Edward Thomas
Dr. Thomas Wood : *True Thomas*
J. O. Parker : *The Life of J. O. Parker*
Mrs. Graves : *History of Harwich Harbour*, Carlyon Hughes
W. F. Crittall and Messrs. Constable : *Fifty Years of Work and Play*, Mr. and Mrs. Crittall
Sir John Ruggles-Brise : *Notes on the East Essex Hunt*, A. W. Ruggles-Brise
The Executors of H. G. Wells : *Mr. Britling Sees it Through*, H. G. Wells
Canon Berridge : *Little Things*
Miss I. Holst : *Gustav Holst*
Messrs. Hodge and Co. : *The Trial of Samuel Herbert Dougal*, ed. F. Tennyson Jesse
L. Woolf : *The Common Reader*, V. Woolf
General Oglander and the Hogarth Press : *Admiral's Widow*
J. Hone and Messrs. Heinemann : *Life of Henry Tonks*
Messrs. Constable and A. P. Watt and Sons : *Journals of Arnold Bennett*
The Oxford University Press : *The Wynne Diaries*, ed. A. Fremantle
The Syndics of the Cambridge University Press : *The Miracles of King Henry VI*, Knox
Messrs. Harrap: *Ego* 2, James Agate
P. P. Eckersley and Jonathan Cape : *The Power behind the Microphone*
John Lane : *The Diary of Dr. Salter*, ed. Thompson

ABBREVIATIONS

E.R.   *Essex Review*
T.E.A.S.   *Transactions of the Essex Archaeological Society*

WARNING

Owing to conditions during the compilation of this book no guarantee is given for the accuracy of the extracts and purists are referred to the original printed sources.

Name's Sake

V. H. FRIEDLAENDER

There are some who say that Essex
Cannot hold her own with Wessex,
That an ampler beauty fills
Town-worn hearts in Cumbrian hills,
Devon combe and Sussex down
Weave a richer poet's crown.

Is there none to praise the shadow
More than substance ? Little Baddow,
Birdbrook, Scarlets, Wivenhoe,
Have you not your names to show ?
Finchingfield and Clavering—
This to play and that to sing.

Margaretting, Margaret Roothing—
Sounds enchanting, ancient, soothing ;
Havering-atte-Bower, Marks Tey,
Hainault, Layer-de-la-Haye,
Vange, High Easter : centuries
Wind in song through names like these.

Lilting numbers, lovely measures ;
Essex, these things are your treasures.
These the untravelled feet may see
On the wings of poetry.
Leave to others other claims :
Beauty's self is in your names !

Essex v. Surrey, 1914

H. G. WELLS : *Mr. Britling Sees it Through*, 1916

" It must be very interesting," said Mr. Britling, " to come over here and pick up these American families of yours on the monuments and tombstones. I doubt though you will find many Hinkinsons in Market Saffron. But lots of this country here has five- or six-hundred-year-old families still flourishing. That's why Essex is so much more genuinely Old England than Surrey, say, or Kent. Round here you'll find Corners and Fairlies, and then you get Capels, and then away down towards Dunmow and Braintree Maynards and Byngs. And then there are oaks and hornbeams in the park about Claverings that have echoed to the howling of wolves and the clank of men in armour. All the old farms here are moated—because of the wolves. Claverings itself is Tudor, and rather fine too. And the cottages still wear thatch. . . . "

He reflected. " Now if you went south of London instead of northward it's all different. You're in a different period, a different society. You're in London suburbs right down to the sea. You'll find no genuine estates left, not of our deep-rooted familiar sort. You'll find millionaires and that sort of people, sitting in the old places. Surrey is full of rich stockbrokers, company-promoters, bookies, judges, newspaper proprietors. Sort of people who fence the paths across their parks. They do something to the old places—I don't know what they do— but instantly the countryside becomes a villadom. And little sub-estates and red-brick villas and art cottages spring up. And a kind of new, hard neatness. And pneumatic tyre and automobile spirit advertisements, great glaring boards by the roadside. And all the poor people are inspected and rushed about until they forget who their grandfathers were. They become villa parasites and odd-job men, and grow basely rich and buy gramophones. This Essex and yonder Surrey are as different as Russia and Germany. But for one American who comes to look at Essex, twenty go to Godalming and Guildford and Dorking and Lewes and Canterbury. Those Surrey people are not properly English at all. They are strenuous. You have to get on or get out. They drill their gardeners, lecture very fast on agricultural efficiency, and have miniature rifle ranges in every village. It's a county of new notice-boards and barbed-wire fences; there's always a policeman round the corner. They dress for dinner. They dress for everything. If a man gets up in the night to look for a burglar he puts on the correct costume—or doesn't go. They got a special scientific system for urging on their tramps. And they lock up their churches on a week-day. Half their soil is hard chalk or a rationalistic sand, only suitable for bunkers and villa foundations. And they play golf in a large, expensive, thorough way because it's the thing to do. . . . Now here in Essex we're as lax as the eighteenth century. We hunt in any old clothes. Our soil is a rich succulent clay; it becomes semi-fluid in winter—when we go about in waders shooting duck. All our finger-posts have been twisted round by facetious men years ago. And we pool our breeds of hens and pigs. Our roses and oaks are wonderful; that alone shows that this is the real England. If I wanted to play golf—which I don't, being a decent Essex man—I should have to motor ten miles into Hertfordshire. And for rheumatics and longevity Surrey can't touch us. This country is a part of the real England—England outside London and outside manufactures. It is one with Wessex and Mercia or old Yorkshire—or for the matter of that with Meath or Lothian. And it's the essential England still. . . ."

The Golden Boye

Essex Session Rolls, County Record Office

On Thursday after the Feast of St. Michael 1565 a writ was delivered to the Sheriff of Essex, to have at the next Sessions, "John Clarke of Abrydge, yeoman, otherwise called the golden boye."

[Golden lads and girls all must,
As chimney-sweepers, come to dust.

SHAKESPEARE]

Richard Cely sends all the News to his Brother George at Calais

A Mediæval Post-bag, ed. L. LYELL, 1934
The Cely Papers, Camden Society, 1900

[The Celys were important members of the continental woollen trade. They owned Bretts Place, Aveley during the second half of the fifteenth century, the last Cely of Bretts dying there in 1494.]

Jesu 1479 (Nov. 11th)

Sir I have been right sick in Essex afore Hallowtide ; I thank God and good diet I am quit there of now ; and in that Season the hawk took a sickness whereof she died at London ; and when I come to London among all my gowns my best black gown was gnawn with " rattons " about the skirts, and i the next money that I reserved for our father was 30*l*. where of I lost 20*s*. in gold, a my soul I wot not where ; this is to write to you of my pain and grief as ye have done to me of yours ; I pray you to come home at this Christmas and by the grace of Jesu we shall be merry after all this " trybelassyon and whexsasion " of sickness. Sir, our cousin Caldwell recommends him and his Wife to you and they thank you of your great Labour in buying of their bankers [seats] they pray that ye will buy them of with flowers and no silk, with six cushions of the same work of the bankers.

Jesu 1479 (Dec. 15th)

Right wellbeloved brother George, I recommend me heartily unto you thanking you of the great kindness that ye showed me at my being with you at Calais, and for your russet gown furred with black lamb that I had in the ship with me, for I trow I had been lost for cold but for it. Sir I delivered the same gown to John Lambe, woolpacker, to convey it to you again and he promised me so to do.

Anno Jesu 1481 (Nov. 5)

Right well beloved brother. . . . I understand that ye have sold your great grey horse, and am right glad thereof, for 2 is as good as 20. A great unfortune is fallen on your bitch, for she had 14 fair whelps, and after she had whelped, she never ate meat, and so she is dead, and all her whelps : but I trust to purvey against your coming as fair and as good to please that gentleman.

I understand ye purpose to be with us for Christmas, and therefore we be right glad, and we shall make merry by the grace of God. . . .

(Nov. 26)

Our mother would that ye would buy for her more green ginger and a quartern saffron.

Belhus

[Belhus came into the possession of the family of Barrett in 1531 and remained there until 1922. The following extracts from their family papers are taken from T. BARRETT-LENNARD : *An Account of the Families of Lennard and Barrett*, 1908.]

From the will of Lord Newburgh, son of Charles Barrett of Belhus, 1643.

Amongst other bequests :—

To my wife—the dymend hoope ring which I usuallie weare.

To my Noble and deare brother Sir Richard Leveson my gold clocke ;

To Chaloner Chute £20 and a bay gelding called Bay Aloffe : and a picture of a pot of flowers which hangs usually in the withdrawing chamber [in London] to my noble and most honoured friend the Ladie Dacres widdowe.

To ffrances now the wife of Benjamin Blackhead, the choyce of any of my night gownes :

He left £130 to his servants, " of which £30 is to be distributed among the undermaids."

[From May 1670 to December 1671, Mr. Dacre Barrett (b. 1653) and his brother Richard (b. 1654), sons of Richard Barrett, completed their education at Paris and Orleans.]

They were under the charge of a tutor and on their return he submitted elaborate accounts of every expense incurred, the whole amounting to £512 0s. 5d. £2 1s. 8d. was paid " For cureing the Lacqueys foot being broken by a cart running over him " and 3s. 4d. " twice for drawing out of Mr. Richard tooth." The party bought fifty pairs of shoes at 4s. a pair. The two boys received lessons in dancing, playing the guitar and the " castaniettes," besides Music, language, philosophy, fencing and tennis. Their "Divertissments" included plays, the opera, etc., and seeing three men broken on the wheel and one shot to death and " we was invited to a Christmas supper, but payed for it 14s."

Meanwhile their sister Anne, being a girl, was having a less interesting time.]

The Hon. Roger North on Anne Barrett

ROGER NORTH (1655-1718) : *The Lives of the Norths*, 1826

I used to make Frequent visits to Bellhouse to my relations there, because it lay near Purfleet, from whence I could walk thither. And this I did more out of respect to a lady, Mistress A. Barrett als Lennard, daughter of Mr. Barrett my cousen german, than any diversion his company afforeded, who though ingenious, and in general of a very good understanding, was of such a morose wilful spirit that it was very fastidious to be in his company, especially considering his infirmities, which had disabled him as to all action ; and he spent his whole time either in bed or in a chair, and was carried from one to the other. But his daughter was bred with my Lady Dacre's own Aunt who was a lady of extraordinary character, and particularly well bred, and of an undaunted spirit. Here she stayed till her father, like a beast, took her away to be buried with him alive in the country ; where by the tyranny of his temper, being always cross & perverse, especially to his children, he had broke her to the greatest degree of submission and obedience that I ever observed. Although she was there for the most part alone, and without company fit for her, she found ways to entertain herself so that her time was not lost. Her more than ordinary wit and fluency of discourse, made her as good company as one would desire in a relation.

It was believed that I made addresses to her, in order to match with her, and I do not wonder at it, because it was notorious that I took frequent and great pleasure in her company. But her fortune, and mine, were not enough to support that outward form of living, according to the esteem of the world, which I thought became the quality I should take her into. Therefore I never made any experiment to

B

know if my service that way would be accepted by her; but applied myself to serve & oblige her by all other ways that fell in my power. In the mean time I cannot omit one passage in the history of this lady, for whom I had so much honour, to show that virtue, early or late, will find a reward beyond what never fails to attend it, I mean (besides a quiet mind), a happy settlement. The old man, upon the revolution of some uncountable perverseness (for he was never friends with all his children at once), fell out with this daughter, & her poor weak sister. It was thought his reason was, that they had mutually given to each other their fortunes (which had been secured to them and not to him), but notwithstanding the merit of so many years slavery to his humour, and an unmatched obedience, he was implacable, and would by all means turn her out of his house to shift for herself as well as she could. And, concurrent with this displeasure, an overture of an honourable match came [with Carew Mildmay, of Marks Hall, Romford], which grew up with it, and as the one was desperate, the other took place, as if Providence had provided a husband to succeed a father. This match I treated for her, adjusted a full jointure & provision for children, and as a father gave her [away], and within a few years an estate fell to her husband in Somersetshire of 600*l*. per annum. She has several sons, and lives happily, and is able to protect her sister, who was to be discarded with her. This I look upon as a happy catastrophe after a desolate life, and I should be glad for the sake of the world (if they deserve so much mercy) that all instances of virtue and vice were as conspicuously remunerated according to their deserts.

[Lord Dacre (Thomas Barrett Lennard) 1717–86, married Anne, daughter of Sir John Pratt, of Seal, Kent. Their only child]

Anne Barbara (Ah bitter day) was snatched away by a violent feaver, just as she was entering into the 10th year of her age.

[Lady Dacre never had another child; but by Elizabeth "Fitzthomas" Lord Dacre had a son whom he made his heir, and a daughter, both of whom were treated as her own by Lady Dacre. Of Miss Lennard, as the girl was called, a friend wrote]

Jan. 12th, 1789. I passed my Christmas with Lady Dacre and Miss Lennard at Belhus very pleasantly. Miss Lennard is by no means handsome, and has had the misfortune of having the jaundice, which has changed a very fine skin to a deep yellow at times, yet she has every accomplishment and goodness of heart to make a rational man happy.

[Thomas, the son, took his part in the affairs of the county, and in 1799 when invasion was threatened by France, raised the Barnstable and Chafford Volunteer Troop of Yeomanry Cavalry. Mrs. Lennard, his wife, worked colours and Lady Dacre wrote a long account of their presentation to her step-daughter who was now married.]

Belhouse Aug. 21st, 1799.

My Dearest Mrs. Hichens

I feel I have so much to tell you that a folio sheet is necessary, tho' I wont answer for filling half of it. I cannot describe how much I was mortified in Your absence, on a day which I persuade myself You would have been highly gratified with. . . . To begin with the Breakfast. The Tables in the Dining parlour were plentifully filled with everything good, such as Beef, Veal, Lamb, Hams, Tongues, and Fowls, potted Meat, Tarts, Sallets, &c &c, Chiefly served upon Plate ; Swan and the Cook had exerted their skill in turning the various sorts of Meat into gimcracks, for instance, one Ham appeared to be a Swan, another an Old Woman resting herself on a Lawn ; Boys getting over Stiles ; A goose swimming, & fish in the Water ; in short I cannot give You a perfect description, but it was all excessively pretty and by what appeared it gave much satisfaction to those it was prepared for : They did not know whether all was to be eaten, as many of the dishes were covered with Lard, but when the Discovery was made, they sliced away and were delighted. The Table was prepared for fourscore : in the Bow window, There was Coffee, & Chocolate, & in the Breakfast Parlour a long table with Tea, and all sorts of Eatables such as Roles, hot Cakes, &c. The Men not only stuffed off what is above described, in the eating way but would have Tea & Coffee brought them, tho there was as much red, & white Wine as they chose, set on the table with the Meat. In short the stuffage continued for at least an hour. We reckoned that at least 150 breakfasted in the above named two rooms. I presented a very fat Buck, and excepting your Brother, there was not a sober man of the party.

Winter

JESSE BERRIDGE (Rector of Little Baddow) : *Little Things,* 1937

I found a sparrow starved and dead—
  The white snow lay on Baddow Hall ;
And I bethought me Jesus said
  Our Father marks the sparrow's fall.
    Saviour, for this thy word divine
    I build in my dark heart a shrine.

With heavy hoof I saw a horse
  Shatter the ice on Cuckoos' pond ;
O break my frozen will perforce
  To drink my love that lies beyond,
    Dear Lord, that would'st not have me be
    Sunless and in captivity.

I saw the beasts at Holy Bread
  Pull at the hay and rest in mire ;
O thou, my shadowy heart, I said,
  Art even as yon cattle-byre.
    Christ, that didst choose their poverty,
    Behold my heart thus needing Thee.

I saw a Maid with child at breast
  Lie down upon a bed of straw,
And sing her little Son to rest
  And round His head her wimple draw ;
    Ah, blessed Maid, my soul is sere
    And dry as death—bring thou Him here !

BATTLESBRIDGE

JAMES AGATE : *Ego 2*, 1936

. . . the lovely unexpected village of Battlesbridge, where, suddenly, in the middle of the inland landscape, arise the masts and brown, close-furled sails of some sea-and-river-going barge.

The Tithe of Milk

MSS. probably early eighteenth century, among the title deeds of the late Mr. C. F. D. Sperling : *E.R.*, vol. xlix

Thomas Mott to be asked whether he remembers the tythe of milk to be paid in the church porch of Pauls belchamp. If yea, by whom, & how long, & whether it was there received in pails or churns or what other vessels.

Knows nothing but that it was paid by Mr. Hammond & carried by Roger Golding, since dead.

The Miller of Foxearth whether he remembers the payment of tythe milk in the church porch of Foxearth, by whom & for what part of the summer.

He paid it 3 Months May June & July every 10th Day Morn & Night : he pour'd it into a Cowl set in the Church Porch at 6 in the Morn & 6 at night : for 2 or 3 Years.

Lord Bayning's Beds, 1635

A Breiff Declaracion touching the state of the Accompts of the Right Honorable Paule Lo : Bayning, Viscount Sudbury, kept by George Pike touching such parcells of his Lordship's Estate as were committed to the care and Government of the Right Honoble the Ladie Viscountess Dorchester his Lordship's Mother by order of the Court of Wardes.

Round MSS., Hist. MSS. Com., 14th Report, 1895

For six peeces of White Chinay to be died and made up for a Bedd at Bentley	30	0	0
For a paire of Vallence bought to send to Bentley in April 1634	2	18	0
For Greene cloth bought then for Bedds for Bentley	34	16	0
Gold and Silver lace for a Purple bedd then	20	8	4
For a Rich Orring [Orange] Tawney damask bed with Vallence Counterpoint Carpet Stooles and Chayres in Oct 1634	97	1	0
For a Flock bed for Mark lane	1	14	0
For yellowe Taffetie and Sateen for Curtins and Vallence for Bentley	15	4	3
For Feathers to fill 5 bedds at Bentley in April 1635	22	17	0

[with other items, total £704   8   6]

" Liberty is a Sweet Thing "

Mr. John Ray, of Black Notley, the father of English botany, to Mr. Courthorpe, 1661

Further Correspondence of John Ray, ed. GUNTHER, 1928

I am now in Essex, where I intend to continue till Bartholomew Day be past. I am as good as resolved not to subscribe the declaration in the Act of Uniformity, and soe can expect no other than the deprivation of my fellowship [of Trinity College, Cambridge]. I must stay hereabouts to make up my accounts, and to dispose of my goods, till about Michaelmas. Many of our ministers in this county will be deprived upon this act, and those the most able and considerable. I shall now cast myself upon Providence and good friends. Liberty is a sweet thing.

Newhall

GIBBS : *The Romance of George Villiers, first Duke of Buckingham*, 1908

[In 1622 Newhall, which had been a royal palace of Henry VIII, passed into the possession of James I's favourite, George Villiers, then Marquess but later Duke of Buckingham. It was from this house that the Duke and Prince Charles set out with disguised beards and the borrowed names of John and Thomas Smith on their wild escapade to view the daughter of the King of Spain. During their stay abroad Buckingham received frequent letters from his devoted wife, of which the following gives details of Newhall, or Beaulieu as it was sometimes called, and of his little daughter Mary or Moll, who was adored not only by her parents but by the King.]

Dear Heart,

. . . indeed I must crave your pardon that I did not write you no more particulars of our pretty Moll. She is very well, I thank God. . . .

She loves dancing extremely, and when the saraband is played, she will get her thumb and finger together, offering to snap ; and then when Tom Duff is sung, then she will shake her apron. She will be excellent at a hat, for if one lay her down she will kick her legs over her head ; but when she is older I hope she will be more modest. Every body says she grows every day more like you than other. You shall have her picture very shortly. I am very glad you have the pearls, and that you like them so well ; and am sure they do not help you to win the ladies' hearts. Yourself is a jewel that will win the hearts of all the women in the world ; but I am confident it is not on their power to win your heart from a heart that is, was, and ever shall be yours till death. . . . When the King went to Newhall it was reported here in town he went to meet you there ; I would they had said truly. My lord I have not yet been to Newhall, but I do intend shortly to go see how forward things are there. The walk to the house is done, and the tennis courts almost done, but the garden is not done nor nothing to the bowling green ; and yet I told Fotherbe, and he told me, he would set men to work presently. But I do warrant you they will all be ready before you come for

Buely. I heard the wall is not very forward yet, and my lady bade me send you word that she is gone down to look how things are there. She says she is about makeing a little river to run through the park, it will be about sixteen feet broad : but she says she wants money. Thus hoping I have obeyed your commands in sending you word of all things you bade me I rest

Your most dutiful wife till death,   K. BUCKINGHAM.

AUBREY, J. : *Brief Lives*
SMITH : *History of the New Hall Community*, n.d.
The Wynne Diaries, vol. 3, 1940

[In 1648 Oliver Cromwell bought the estate with a derisive payment of 5s., but twelve years later it, with the Dukedom of Albemarle, was part of the reward given to General Monk who had engineered the return of Charles II to the throne.]

Aubrey gives this account of Monk's marriage.

George Monk was a strong, lusty well-sett young fellow, and at the beginning of the late civill warres, he came over to the king's side, where he had command. He was taken prisoner by the Parliament forces, and kept in the Tower, where his semstress, Nan Clarges (a blacksmith's daughter) was kind to him ; in a double capacity. It must be remembered that he was then in want for he was forgotten and neglected at Court, and they did not think of exchanging him, and she assisted him. Here she was gott with child. She was not at all handsome, nor cleanly. Her mother was one of the five woeman barbers.

" Her brother Thomas Clarges, came a ship-board to G.M. and told him his sister was brought to bed. 'Of what ?' sayd he. 'Of a Son.' 'Why then' sayd he 'she is my Wife.' He had only this child."

[According to a note in *Pepys's Diary* General Monk was married in 1652 to Anne Clarges, daughter of his regimental farrier ; the son was born in the following year and suckled by Honour Mills, a vendor of apples and oysters. He succeeded his father as Duke of Albemarle, but Pepys and others suspected his legitimacy as Anne had married Thomas Ratford in 1632 and no certificate of his death had ever appeared, though she was separated from him in 1649.

Pepys had a poor opinion of the Duchess, calling her " a plain homely dowdy," " an ill-looking and ill-natured woman " and " a slut and a drudge." He also thought little of the Duke, a typical comment being that of 28 December, 1663 : " Went and spoke with the Duke of Albemarle about his wound at Newhall, but I find him a heavy dull man, methinks, by his answers to me." Nothing further is known about the wound.

At the end of the eighteenth century New Hall was bought by the Canonesses of the Holy Sepulchre, who had fled to England from Liége in 1799. The *Gentleman's Magazine* for 1800 records that the noble double avenue of limes, a mile long, " were sold at 8s. a tree to Mr. Cotes, coal and timber merchant of Chelmsford, who by selling them to turners, and to make bedsteads, etc., for the barracks, is said to have cleared £500. The scene of Harry's intrigues and pleasures, is now the retreat of fifty religious virgins under a lady abbess, who has added to their number young ladies of the first families as boarders for instruction."

One of these young ladies was Miss Harriet Wynne, who with her sister Justine was a pupil at New Hall from 1800 to 1804. Their parents had recently died, and they lived with their elder sister Eugenia in London, Elizabeth, or Betsy, the eldest of the family being the wife of Captain Thomas Fremantle of the Royal Navy. Elizabeth, Eugenia and Harriet were all life-long diarists, and the latter's record of life at New Hall nearly 150 years ago shows that schoolgirls' emotions are changeless.

The last days of her education were filled with a *schwärmerei* for one of the nuns. Mother Agatha, the object of her devotion, was born at Witham nearby, but had entered the Community at Liège, and received the habit when only fourteen years of age. She was mainly in charge of the pupils, possessed a beautiful voice, and was both learned and lovable.]

Sunday, 3rd June, 1804. I was greatly disappointed in going to tea to Mother Subprioress for instead of meeting Mother Agatha or Sister Sales, Sister (A) made her appearance. I was so provoked that I could have killed them.

Monday, 30th July. I went to Confession and did not mention ——. M.A. was all kindness to me. After Vespers she came down and preached me so delightful a sermon that I could have eat her up.

Sunday, 12th August. I did not go to High Mass. I had a letter from Betsey and Justina during dinner. They are very anxious about me [on account of the threatened invasion] and wish me to go soon. Mother Agatha payed me a short and *sweet* visit before Angelus ; I was in the Yellow room sitting on my bed.   We were as tender as usual.   She no sooner left me than I set out such howlings that I felt quite alarmed at myself.

Tuesday, 14th August.   Spoke to M.A. in the morning ; she was all kindness to me and made me promise to write to her.   The nuns are to go in a retreat on Thursday evening and I grieved to say Mother Agatha is one of them.

Wednesday, 15th August.   The Assumption the mass went very well.   The sermon we had kept us from dining till twelve therefore we had no lecture.   Mother Agatha came down at one and invited me to tea ; she reminded me of our walk up and down the Avenue when she shewed me the way ; we both regretted the retreat beginning tomorrow ; but patience must be my resource.   At two I went to tea ; we spent our time very agreably, though I own I felt low spirited. She promised to come to me again but never did.   Sister Elizabeth asked her about the hair, *her* answer was I would not be proper, besides she had cut it lately so close that she was sure she could not get a bit.

Thursday, 16th August.   This was a dull and melancholy day and I felt more than it was possible for any creature to do. I saw M.A. in the morning twice.   She said nothing to me particular, but promised to see me before she went in retreat. I practised from a quarter to three till the half hour after four ; when I was summoned to Mother Agatha who was waiting for me in the refectory.   I went in and found Sister Regis with her.   I remained in the little kitchin until their parley was over and Sister Regis with her usual *smile* ushered me in. Several pensioners came in the room and this provoked my darling M.A. who locked the door.   She did not say much to me but what she did went to my very heart.   I cannot express what I felt when I was with her ; I could not speak ; she was rather inclined to silence.   At last the cruel moment arrived when the terrible *Adieu* was pronounced, but M.A.'s embrace was sweet, she no sooner left the room than I began to cry most desperately.   I went upstairs and Euleston got me some tea destitute of sugar, to dry my weeps, she remained with me until she went to Mr. Holder.   I continued to cry to supper. I went to bed soon and weeped till they came to bed.   I then behaved very well but did not sleep well.

The Custom of the Manor of Borley in the Middle Ages

G. G. COULTON : *The Medieval Village*, 1931 ; quoting VINOGRADOFF : *Villainage*, 1892

And let it be known that when he, the villain, with other customers shall have done cutting the hay on the meadow in Raneholm, they will receive by custom three quarters of wheat for baking bread, and one ram of the price of eighteen pence, and one pat of butter, and one piece of cheese of the second sort from the lord's dairy, and salt, and oatmeal for cooking a stew, and all the morning milk from all the cows in the dairy, and for every day a load of hay. He may also take as much grass as he is able to lift on the point of his scythe. And when the mown grass is carried away, he has the right to one cart. And he is bound to carry sheaves, and for each service of this kind he will receive one sheaf called " mene-sheaf." And whenever he is sent to carry anything with his cart, he shall have oats, as usual, so much, namely, as he can thrice take with his hand.

A Braintree Traitor ?

Letters and Papers of Henry VIII, ed. GAIRDNER, vol. xi

On the 10th Sept., 1536, in the presence of Guill. le Fla-
mencq : and five others, echevins of the *pays de l'Angle*, one
names Joen Aelleen, a prisoner, native of Brantry in England,
as he says, was examined and said he and his wife had come to
serve the masons of Calais ; and when after Easter last they
did not work, he returned and they enrolled themselves under
the captain of Tournehen, whom they served two months.
He acknowledges having received from his captain two pieces
of gold, besides sharing sometimes in booty taken from the
French. After two months he went to St. Omer, and put
himself on the roll of Mons de Curelu and they were under
him about three weeks, and received from him about two
pieces of gold. Afterwards they went to Boulougne with a
passport they had from Captain de Curelu, when the Captain
of Boulougne offered each a gold crown if they would take
the field where he pleased ; but they refused, and came back
to Querseque and the said prisoner came back with the rest
to the castle of Antinghes. During this time he acknowledges
he was sent by his captain through the English pale to L'Angle
to examine the roads, with a halter in his sleeve to take any
horse or other beast he might find.

> [*Braintree boys, brave boys.*
> *Bocking boys, rats.*
> *Church Street, puppy dogs,*
> *High Garrett, cats.*
>
> Old Rhyme, *Essex Review*, vol. iii]

A " Gatherer-oopp " of Horse Hairs

Essex Sessions Rolls, Hist. MSS. Com., 10th Report, 1885

1572. Licence granted to Richard Anderson of Branklie
co. Essex, labourer, beinge verie aged poore and impotente,

to travel the country and gain his livelihood by gathering oopp of horse heers steers heer and cowes heer within the counties of Essex, Kent, Suffolke and Norfolk, and selling the same to such persons as make hayers and other things thereof.

Benjamin Allen, 1666–1738

of The Great House, Braintree, Doctor of Medicine and Naturalist.
Some notes from his Commonplace Books
Essex Naturalist, vols. xvi, xvii, ed. MILLER CHRISTY

1693. A strange changeable summer and winter, more so than ever remembered by an old man at Leighs. Fermentative quality of the air layd aside ; liquors would not work ; yeast half-a-crown a quart. Hens layd no eggs ; those that kept 50 hens had not 3 eggs layd in a week.

1699. The first year of the return of warm summers. this year there was great sickness among horses, so that ye King could not get horses to go to Newmarket.

1708. Universal colds in horses, as in K. W (illiam)'s time. Only mine and one more escaped in our Hundred, as far as I could hear, but many dyed.

Sir William Daws, now Archbishop of York, had a stubborn ague, ever returning. It tir'd him and fainted him, and he then drank of our steel'd water at Wethersfield, but was at last cured by taking the Peruvian bark every morning for six weeks or two months, as he told me himself.

[A further entry refers to the time when "my daughter Mary was courted by Mr. ——, supposed to be a Papist (his sister being a profest one)." One day when the supposed Papist was present, Allen's son, Benjamin, coming into the room, was seized with a sudden illness. This was so clearly a warning from Heaven that the Doctor could do no less than dismiss the suitor for his daughter's hand, with the result that within two days his son recovered his health. The daughter, however, never married.

Allen noted on two separate occasions that Queen Anne died on the day on which an Act against dissenters and another for transporting poor children came into force—evidently cause and effect.]

Learning and Leather: Local Industries in 1860

MR. AND MRS. F. H. CRITTALL, *Fifty Years of Work and Play*, 1934

Braintree was a town of small craftsmen. There were thirty-two boot and shoe makers, ten blacksmiths, four whitesmiths, four ironmongers, a stay-maker, and four straw-hat makers. There were also twelve academies and schools in Braintree and Bocking, seven of which took in boarders. In addition, there were six public schools. There was a town missionary, a lath render, a music professor, and a whip-maker, and the larger and ancient silk works of Courtaulds and Warners were as busy then as they are today.

A Lusty Chelmsford Maiden

Kemps nine daies wonder, Performed in a daunce from London
to Norwich, 1600

Camden Society, 1840

At Chelmsford, a Mayde not passing foureteene yeares of
age, dwelling with one Sudley, my kind friend, made request
to her Master and Dame that she might daunce the Morrice
with me in a great large roome.   They being intreated, I was
soone wonne to fit her with bels ; beside she would have the
olde fashion, with napking on her armes ; and to our iumps
we fell.   A whole houre she held out ; but then being ready
to lye downe I left her off ; but this much to her praise, I
would have challenged the strongest man in Chelmsford, and
amongst many I thinke few would have done so much.

The Mildmays of Moulsham

MILDMAY, H. A. ST. J. : *A Brief Memoir of the Mildmay Family,* 1913

[When Henry VIII came to the throne old Thomas Mildmay, of
Chelmsford, sold goods from a stall every Wednesday, but Thomas his
son entered the King's service and soon acquired wealth and position
as a Commissioner for the dissolution of monasteries.   By 1540 he was
the owner of the Manor of Moulsham (1800 acres and a watermill,
previously held by the Monastery of St. Peter, Westminster), where he
proceeded to erect a mansion house which was accounted the greatest
esquire's building in the County of Essex, though it must be remembered that he had 15 children to house.   He died in 1566—Sir Thomas,
Auditor of the Court of Augmentations—and in his will left £40 for a
stone monument " within the church wall at Chelmsford, engraven
with my arms and those of my wife, with the pictures of both and 15
children, one half men children and one half women children " and a
Latin inscription, which has been translated as follows.]

Trans. E.A.S., Vol. 1–2, 1863

Here are seen graven the effigies of
Thomas Mildmay and Avice his wife :
But within their remains lie at peace.

He was a renouned Esquire,
She a daughter, and lovely branch of William Gernon, Esquire,
They had fifteen pledges of their prosperous love,
Seven whereof were females,
Eight are males.
Afterwards, in the year of our Lord, 1557,
And in the morning on the 16th day of September,
Avice returned to that dust
From which she had originally sprung.
And
On the 10th day of the calends of October,
In the ninth year following
The unrelenting King of terrors
Triumphed over Thomas.

[Sir Walter Mildmay, brother of the Auditor, founded Emmanuel College, Cambridge. He was so much of a Puritan that he made the Chapel (now the Library) stand N. and S. instead of E. and W. This was not pleasing to Queen Elizabeth, who said to him when he came to Court :—" Sir Walter, I hear you have erected a puritan foundation." " No, Madam," replied he, " far be it from me to countenance anything contrary to your established laws, but I have set an acorn, which when it comes to be an oak, God alone knows what will be the fruit of it." The chapel was not consecrated and there were early reports of misbehaviour there, the students lolling on forms and talking aloud and pledging each other in bumpers at the Sacrament.

A later Mildmay, Sir Henry, was Master of the Jewel Office under James I and Charles I and in October 1638 the latter King " waited on by the Lords and the rest of the Court went to Chensford and the next day to Mousum (Moulsham) to Sir Henry Mildma's where the Queen Mother (Marie de' Medici, Charles's mother-in-law) had been lodged the night before. Shee mett hym in the Hall, where after the King had bowed towards the hemme of her garment then rising towards her hand kissed her who held him in a great while uppon her neck without speaking to him."

On the outbreak of the Civil War Sir Henry accompanied the King with his army on the borders of Scotland and wrote in laudatory terms of His Majesty :—" Our blessed Master is in perfect health, and the most active and vigilant Prince in his affairs that I think lives " but a year or two later he was actively aiding the Parliamentary side and was one of the judges at the trial of the King, though he did not sign the death warrant, nor was he present when the sentence of death was pronounced. He surrendered to the Commonwealth the treasure under his charge in the Jewel House, which included " two Crowns called the King and the Queene's Crowns, and a third called the Crowne of King Edward the sixth." " As also the Gold and Silver Plate and divers vessels of Christall and Aggats . . . amounting in whole to above £13,000."

The result of these activities was, that on the Restoration, he was tried and condemned to be drawn on a sledge yearly, on the 27th of January, a rope round his neck, to Tyburn and thence to the Tower to be confined for life, and was degraded from his honours and titles.

He petitioned the House of Lords that this sentence should not be carried out, claiming that he only attended the trial of the King in an endeavour to protect his Master, and annexed a certificate from Dr. E. Warner that he was suffering from a rupture, and that if the sentence of drawing on a sledge from the Tower to Tyburn were put in execution it would endanger his life, but it was of no avail, for Pepys enters 27 January, 1661-2 :—" we met with three sleddes standing there to carry my Lord Mousson, Sir Henry Mildmay, and another to the gallows and back again with ropes round their necks which is to be repeated every year, this being the day of their sentencing the King."

His youngest brother Anthony, a member of the household of Charles I, also went over to the side of the Commonwealth and was granted custody of the Duke of Gloucester and Princess Elizabeth after the execution of their father. The diary of the third brother, Humphrey, is reprinted under *Danbury*.

Few of the Mildmays were popular, and in the will of Philip, Earl of Pembroke, there is this clause :—"Seeing that I did menace a certain Henry Mildmay but did not thrash him, I leave the sum of £50 sterling to the lacquey that shall pay my debt." Those familiar with the Autobiography of Sir John Bramston will also recall the enmity between him and Henry Mildmay of Graces, and of the latter's dastardly plot against the Lord Chief Justice.

Carew Mildmay, of Marks Hall, Romford, is said to have been the last of the Mildmays in the direct line. He died in 1784 in his 94th year and used to say that he remembered killing a woodcock on the site of Conduit Street in London, then open country. Horace Walpole wrote in 1765 : " Mr. Chute has quitted the bed today for the first time for about five weeks. He was near relapsing, for old Mildmay, whose lungs, and memory, and tongue will never wear out, talked to him the other night from eight till half an hour after ten on the poor bill, but he has been more comfortable with Lord Dacre and me this evening."

Meanwhile Moulsham Hall had passed to another branch of the family, having been rebuilt at the beginning of the eighteenth century at a cost of £70,000. In 1803 it was found necessary to throw up military works against Napoleon's threatened invasion within 400 yards of the house, 1500 people being employed in the construction. Sir

Henry Mildmay was offered compensation at the rate of £400 a year, but as the result of a vigorous protest in the House of Commons this was raised to £1300 for one year and £600 for the remainder. The house was never re-occupied and finally pulled down in 1816, probably to his great relief as he had previously been compelled by his marriage settlement to live there for at least three months in each year.]

"A Pure Theife"

Letters from Chelmsford Gaol, 1674

Verney Letters, Vol. 4, 1899

[That the gentleman turned highwayman is not entirely a creation of the romantic novelists is shown by the career of Dick Hals, a cousin of the Verneys of East Claydon in Buckinghamshire. He had served with distinction in the Navy during the Dutch Wars, but being either unwilling or unable to obtain further employment he had taken to a life of crime and in 1674 found himself in Chelmsford Gaol. He was already acquainted with the inside of Newgate and other places of confinement and was ready to turn King's evidence to obtain his release. The following letters were written to his cousin, Sir Ralph Verney.]

June 22, 1674. When I came into this gaole, I was resoulved to die unknowne to my frendes, but Providence orderinge itt otherwayes, to my greate advantage, for althowe I am be banished, itt is but what I should have courted iff left to my owne dispose, being assured that England, Ireland or Scotland are not places for me to rayse my fortune in, soe that to be sent, as I am promised, by that noble gentleman, Esquire Cheeke, into Flanders, Holland, France or Spaine, is the compleate sume of my desires or ambition.

July 26, 1674. All the miseries which attend humanity have fallen on my head. That I was soe weake, on promise of life, to discover others, and yett by the severitie of my new masters, the Judges, to be tyed up for my good service, Could they not as well have pressed me or hanged in my state of inocency, I meane, while I was a pure theife, without blott or blemish as to make me stincke in the nostrills of my ould assosiates, and then out of love to hange me for my new service to my new masters.

August 11, 1674. I am ashamed to discover my weakenesse

unto you, but I must. The sight of the executioner, who is still keept in the house in expectation of my execution on Monday next, is the greatest torment to me in the world, worse then death itselfe.

[Dick escaped the gallows next Monday and in the course of the next five years was once more in gaol; turned up at a festive family wedding (though the previous year he had travelled down to Claydon "in a cart with a Cooke mayd"); and was appointed a Baly "but dos not dou no duty"; before finally mounting the cart at Tyburn in 1685.]

EDWARD THOMAS : *Collected Poems*

If I should ever by chance grow rich
I'll buy Codham, Cockridden, and Childerditch,
Roses, Pyrgo, and Lapwater,
And let them all to my elder daughter.
The rent I shall ask of her shall be only
Each year's first violets, white and lonely,
The first primroses and orchises—
She must find them before I do, that is.
But if she finds a blossom on furze
Without rent they shall all for ever be hers,
Whenever I am sufficiently rich :
Codham, Cockridden, and Childerditch,
Roses, Pyrgo and Lapwater—
I shall give them all to my elder daughter.

[For the younger daughter's dower, and the son's, see Havering-atte-Bower and Margaretting.]

An Old Chingford Custom

The Gentleman's Magazine, 1790, Part 2

Bee it rememb'red, that the three-and-twentieth day of October, in the yeare of our Lord 1659, came Samuell Haddon, and Mary his wife, Edmond Cotster, his man-servant, and Mathew Walle, his maide-servant, to the parsonage of Chingford, at the commaund of Thomas Wytham, Master of Artes, and rector of the said parsonage. The said Samuell Haddon did his homage there, and paid his reliefe in maner and forme as hereafter followeth, for one tenement at Chingford that is called Scottes Mayhewes, alias Brendwood, which was lately purchased of Daniell Thelwel, Esq. First, the said Samuell did blow three blastes with a horne at the said parsonage, and afterwards recieved of the said Thomas Wytham, a chicken for his hawke, a peck of oates for his horse, a loafe of bread for his greyhound, and afterward received his dinner for himselfe, and also his wyfe, his man and his maide. The maner of his cominge to the said parsonage was on horseback, with his hawke on his fist, and his greyhound in his slippe. And after dinner blew three blastes with his horne at the said parsonage, and then paid twelve pence of the lawfull money of England for his relief, and so departed. All these seremoneys were done for the homage and releife of the said tenement at Chingford Hatch, called Scottes Mayhews, alias Brendwood, as before hath beene accustomed to be donne time out of mind.

Witnesses to the performances of the seremoneyes aforesaid,
    Ralphe Delle,
    Jo. Hette,
    John Woodward.

CLACTON

JAMES AGATE : *Ego 2*, 1936

Nothing that I know of can compare with the bosoms of those burnished doves which are Clacton's landladies. They live in houses coloured to match, little houses whose façades have all the chromatic delight of lemon pudding, raspberry sauce, and delicate sweets in blue and green. Stand on that grassy verge which keeps the ocean at arm's length and you have the choice of two pleasures. Face east and you behold "little ships on the crumpled sea, sailing so grand." Face west and you watch young hopeful, aged six, doing justice to his father's wholly lamentable bowling. The probability is that you will combine both joys and simultaneously scan the horizon and with the back of your pants intercept young hopeful's boundary hit. . . . The hub of Clacton is its pier. Walk to the end of this, and there, like as not, you will find the *Laguna Belle*, once known as the *Southend Belle*, and with a history of heroic service in the Dardanelles. She has just brought passengers from London—three glad hours, and it seems not an hour of that supreme and supernal joy which, Swinburne tells us, revives in remembrance the sea-bird's heart in a boy. But the great poet said nothing of the supreme and supernal melancholy if it is the return journey from Clacton you are making, and the joys are left behind.

The Moat House Murder, 1899

The Trial of Samuel Herbert Dougal, 1928, ed. F. TENNYSON JESSE

The one thing that stands out clearly about poor Camille Holland is that she was a perfect example of that type of human being—nearly always a woman—whom one may call the born murderee—a type that the potential murderer is quick to recognise. Hedged in by the conventions and restrictions of her upbringing and her religion, she had retained her virtue up to an age when it would be reasonable to think it might have been safe, and yet the convictions of a lifetime were thrown away by her at the bidding of a coarse, vulgar man who was her social inferior. She feared and distrusted him, and yet she went with him into an isolation so complete that death had removed her from it for four years before any inquiry was set on foot as to her fate.

For the first months after her death Dougal seems to have been extremely popular in the neighbourhood—as a bluff, genial, talkative man. Had he been able to restrain his amours within the not at all narrow limits of the not very exiguous circle in which he moved, he might have been living yet, but it was unwise of him to seduce one sister in front of another, and to deny paternity when confronted with affiliation orders, both of which things he did.

In his vulgar gross way he had some of the tastes attributed to the more dissolute Roman Emperors. He liked a touch of an orgy about his doings, and strange tales got about of bicycling lessons given in the field to girls who rode machines in a state of nature. What a picture—in that clayey, lumpy field, the clayey, lumpy girls, naked, astride that unromantic object, a bicycle, and Dougal, gross and vital, cheering on these bucolic improprieties.

Many of the rumours were doubtless incorrect, but there is no question about his relations with women during this period that his wife was still in the house with him. There is a letter extant, as an answer to an advertisement, and runs as follows :

" Miss L.,—I am in want of some one to look to my wants during the absence of my wife who is frequently away from home, should like one of a cheerful disposition and young. This is a farmhouse and a jolly English home. . . . "

Many women who did not have to be brought into the case were nursing Dougal's children at the time of his trial for the murder of Camille Holland and to one of them he wrote from Chelmsford prison :

I daresay the girls have received their notices, etc., to attend next Monday at Chelmsford, have they not ? There will be several from about there, and it would be a good idea to club together and hire a trap and drive all the way. It is a delightful drive through undulating country, and at this time of year it would be a veritable treat for them all. I was thinking of a child (Daughter) born on the 11th of this month might be named " Draga " after the poor Queen of Servia assassinated on that day ; what a dreadful piece of business ! When you feel like it, please drop me a few lines and let me know how you are.

Coxhall Wise and Coxhall Foolish

Fuller's Worthies, 1662
HARVEY : *Ballads, Sons and Rhymes of East Anglia, 1936*

" JOHN GODARD (wherever born) had his best being at Cogshall in this County, where he became a Cistercian Monke (*c.* 1250). Great was his skill in Arithmetick and Mathematicks, a Science which had lain long asleep in the World, and now first began to open its eyes again. He wrot many certain Treatises thereof, and dedicated them unto *Ralph* Abbot of *Cogshall*."

[Of *Ralph* himself (Abbot 1207–18) Fuller writes.]

" He was a man *Incredibilis frugalitatis & parsimoniae*, but withall of great learning and abilities."

[His *Chronicles* extend from 1066 to 1224, the most interesting part of them being his account of the Holy Land where he speaks from personal knowledge. He was shut up in Jerusalem itself, and was wounded there when Saladin's army besieged it ; for, so he affirms.]

" The face of him who relates these things, was wounded by an arrow, which pierced through the middle of his nose, and although the shaft was extracted, the iron head remains to this day." (DUNKIN, *Monumenta Anglicana.* 1851.)

[Another Coggeshall Worthy is Bishop Jeggon (1550–1617) " our short, fat, lord bishop of Norfolk." Born there of poor parentage he went to Cambridge by way of the local Grammar School, and in 1590 was appointed Master of Corpus Christi, or Bennett, College. He freed the College from debt but had a reputation for miserliness and is said to have obtained the money for repairing the building by inflicting extortionate fines on the undergraduates. A student wag wrote.]

Doctor John Jeggon, of Bennet Colege, Master,
Broke the scholar's heads, and gave the Hall plaister.

[Despite these learned men Coggeshall folk have a reputation like the people of Gotham. A " Coxhall job " has been proverbial for several hundred years. The most interesting concern the church. The townsfolk were dissatisfied with its position and decided to move it. They took off their coats, laid them on the ground, went round to the other side of the building, and pushed hard. When they thought they had gone far enough they came back for their clothes and found they had disappeared. " We must have pushed the church on top of them," they said. Although German bombs wrecked the church in 1940, no trace of the garments was found.]

From the Diary of Joseph Bufton of Coggeshall

Trans. EA.S., vol. 1, 1858.

The charges of my Sister Elizabeth's Burial, April 18, 1666.

Two gall. sack, 4 of clarret	£1 11 6
A barrell of beere	0 11 0
Nine pair of gloves	0 17 0
Five pound of sugar	0 5 0
For ye Buriall	0 2 6
For a coffin	0 8 0
	£3 15 0

July 16, 1678. My Brother John and his wife both took ship at London, to go into Ireland. After w*ch* we heard not of them till the 10th of September, on which day Goodman Lay received a Letter from his daughter, w*ch* I saw and read, whereby we understood they were *six weeks* upon the water.

1680. A new Pillory was set up in Coxhall.

1681. There was a man, a stranger, whipt up Church Street, at ye cart's tail.

Coggeshall Bells.

Nov. 8, 1681. Three Bells were run in Mr Ennow's barn, and the other three Dec. 23, 1681.

In Sep. 1682, the 6th Bell and 3rd Bell were new run at Colchester.

In April, 1683, the 5th Bell was carried to Colchester, and there was made thereof a little bell, less than the least before.

In May, 1692, the great bell was carried to London, to be new shot, and the rest were chipt to make them tuneable.

In Jan., 1694, the 4th bell was split and carried to Sudbury, to be new shot, and brought home about May 7, 1694. Then it was made too little, and was carried to Sudbury, to be new shot and made bigger. And was brought home about June 18, 1694 ; and were first rung after that June 22, 1694.

1682. There was a Ducking stoole set up in a Church pond.

Ye widdow Mootome paid £15.0.0, because she had a bastard ; £10.0.0 of it was given to ye poore.

In the months of July and August, 1684, Coxhall Church was whited and painted.

1685. The first wife of Mr. Boys was buried ; 6 Gentle-women carried up ye Pall, with white hoods and night-gowns ; and Mr. Livermore preached at her funeral ; and I was gone to London.

1686. A daughter of John Church, Singlewoman, was buried, and a garland hung up in ye Church.

About March the Twentyeth, 1686, the Meal men first began to come to Coxhall Market, and had their meals cryed 15 pounds for a shilling, and ye bran was taken out and 14 pound of fine flour for 14*d*.

The Poore that take Collection had badges given them to wear, w*ch* was a P & C cut out in blew cloth.

A new clock was set up at ye Market house, made at London, said to cost 23 pounds.

Jan. 29, 87/8. Prayers were read in ye Church for Queen Mary, upon ye account of her being with child.

June 10, 1688. K. James had a son borne.

February 14, 1689. There was a day of Thanksgiving kept all over the nation, by order of ye Convention (as there was in London 14 days before), for our great deliverance from Popery and Slavery, by ye coming of ye Prince of Orange ; and the same day at Coxall they made a shift to ring ye bells after a fashion [as noted above, they were in the process of being recast] and after Sermon ye effigies of a Pope was carried about ye Town, and at night burnt in a Bonfire. And feb. 21, 1689, King William and Mary were proclaimed at Coxhall (it being Thursday). The Coroner came and it was a Bayliff read ye Proclamation, and a great many guns were shot off here that day, and bonfires made at night.

April 11, being Thursday, King William and Queen Mary were crowned at Westminster. On ye same day, at Coxhall, a garland was made, and oranges hung on it, and carried about ye towne, and a drum beat before it, and ye bells were rung so well as they could ring them, and a great many bonfires were made at night.

King William went through Kelvedon May 1, 1691. And againe March 4, 1692. And againe October 20, 1692. And then he stayed and dined at the Angell. He went through again March the 24, 1693, and back againe through Kelvedon March 28, 1693. And he went through againe October 30, 1693.

There was 6 times, but I find no more that I recorded. But, in 1700, he was at Colchester, I think it was in October, and then he went through Kelvedon, as he went to London. And that makes 7 times.

September 8, 1692, being Thursday, and the same day that Jacob Cox dyed, about 2 o'clock, there was an earthquake at Coxall, and many towns beside hereabouts, and at London and severall other countries, we heard, and the news letter said it was at ye same time in holland, and ye rest of ye provinces in ye Netherlands. I was in our garret at that time, and heard the house crack, and perceived it shake, and was afraid it would fall, and therefore ran down staires.

May 1, 1693. The soldiers set up a may pole at ye woollpack door.

In the latter end of May, 1693, the Poor had Badges given them to wear, which tis said, were made of Pewter, and Coggeshall Poor, 1693, set upon them.*

In the yeare 1693, A new pound was set up on Grange hill, and the Shambles repaired.

1693. The poor did rise because the Bakers would not bake, because some of their bread was cut out the day before, for being too light.

---

* Aubrey, in his *Anecdotes and Traditions* (Camden Society) notes : Before the Civil Warre I remember Tom a'Bedlams went about a begging. They had been such as had been in Bedlam and there recovered, and come to some degree of sobernesse, and when they were licensed to goe out they had on their lefte arme an armilea of tinne (printed), about three inches breadth which was sordered on.

Gloves at my Father's Buriall :—1695.

	£	s	d
Ten pr of Corderant	£1	0	0
Two pr sheep	0	2	0
Three pr kid	0	6	0
Three pr lamb	0	3	0
	£1	11	0

Oct. the 8th, 1695. The poor did rise at Coxall, in ye evening, to hinder ye carrying away of corne. And Jonathan Cable beat a drum to gather them together, for which he was carried before a Justice, but not sent to Jaile. The poor did rise at Colchester, and other places, about ye same time, and it was said burnt several waggons.

1696. Peter's well was very well repaired by ye Constables.

1697. There were a great many fighting cocks carried through Coxhall, on horseback, in linnen baggs or clothes.

July 13, 1699. The widow Comon was put into the river to see if she wold sink, because she was suspected to be a witch —and she did not sink, but swim.

And she was tryed again July 19th, and then she swam again, and did not sink.

July 24, 1699. The widow Comon was tryed a third time by putting her into the river, and she swum and did not sink.

Dec. 27th, 99. The widow Comon, that was counted a witch, was buried.

From the Household Books of John, Lord Howard, later 1st Duke of Norfolk, 1481-84

Roxburghe Club, 1844, ED. COLLIER

[The Duke's principal residence was Stoke Nayland in Suffolk, but he was Constable of Colchester from 1461 until his death on Bosworth Field in 1485 and some of his expenditures in Essex may be of interest. Those incurred in fitting out the Fleet at Harwich in 1481 will be found on p. 82.]

1481. The costes whyl my Lord was a huntynge at Weveno, and all the weye.

At Weveno.

Item, the 3*de* day of Septembre, for beefe 2*s*. 6*d*. For bred 2*s*. 2*d*. For otte mele, mustard, peper, and saffron 4*d*. For helping in the kechyn 1*d*. For beddes at Mylbornys 2*d*. For the washinge of the wyffes nappry 2*d*.

At Bentle Parke.

The 4th day of Septembre for bred 12*d*. For brekfaste in the mornynge 2*s*.

At Seynt Ossyis.

The 5th day of Septembre, for the parers of saffron 4*d*. To the harper 4*d*. To the Abbuttes coke [Abbott's cook] 20*d*. To the pantry and the seler 2*s*.

Item, my Lord gaff to the parker at Elmysted at his beying there   5*s*.

At Weveno, homward.

The 6th day of Septembre, To 3 botemen for bryngynge my Lord up from Weveno to Seynt Ossyis 20*d*. Item, for my Lordes offerynge at Seynt Osy 4*d*. For bere for my Lordes dener 2*d*. For the taborettes, and odyr for brekfaste 8*d*.

And on Mykelmes day . . .

Willm Davyes, prest of Neylond, for bordyng of litel Richard, synger.

Rychard Tornour, carpenter.

Md. that the 22 day of Octobre, my Lord made covenaunt with Rychard Tornour, carpenter, that he schal take downe my Lordes new howse at Colchester, and lay it in my Lordes barnes, and my Lord schal cary yt to Stoke at Candelmesse, and the said Rychard schal rere it and sett yt up there, as my Lord schal apointe him, and he schal garnysh yt accordynge to his fyrst covenaunte, and for his covenaunt he schal have 46s. 8d., and gef he do his parte wele, and deserve more, he schal have as Mayster Brame wyl say that he deservyth.

Item, my Lord payd to the flecher of Colchester, for federunge and pecyng of his schaftes [arrows]   8d.

[November] my Lord gave Thomas Terell, that he should not sew [sue] the vecory of Wormyngford, 4 yerdes of sateyn.

And on Tewisday night, the 27 day of November, I rekyned with my Lord, and he sed I shulde how him 5s. 4d., and I said but 4s. 8d., where of I was alowed for my wages 4d., and 2s. 8d., befor. Summa 6s. 8d.   So should rest, be my Lordes rekyning, in my hand 16d., and I say but 8d. wherfor the percillis [parcels] above wreten schal schew

And the same nyght I rec. of my Lord upon a new rekyning
                                                            38s.

[Lord Howard spent Christmas, or as it is written in the Accounts, Xpemes, at his house at the Hithe, Colchester.]

Item, for the children of the Chapel, on Xpemes day for ther patins and poyntes   12d.
Item, your offeryng at the church   10d.
Item, for fesantes to maister Gorge   6d.
Item, the 26 day of December, my Lord toke to the Plaiers of Kokesale   3s. 4d.
Item to the mynstrel was here on Xpemes day   20d.
Item, to the Plaiers of Hadley, and the olde man and 2 children
                                                            6s. 8d.
Item, to the trompetz for a rewarde   6s. 8d.
And for a lytel horne that my Lady sent to my yong Maister Howarde   3s.

The 7 day Januare [1482]
Item, to a man broght veneson from Colom [Colne] Parke
                                                            20d.
Item, to the Plaiers of Esterforde [Kelvedon]   3s. 4d.
Thomas,   } Item, I paid for 4 yerdes narowe cloth for Tomas
the harper }   for his lyard [grey] gown   5s. 8d.

45

[February] Item, to Barker of Kolcester for a tabul   7s. 4d.

[March] Item, I toke to the clokke maker of Kolcester for emendyng the clokke   2s. 4d.

[Richard Tornor] Item, my Lord made covenaunt with Rychard Tornor to make his new wall at Colchester ; and the seyde Rychard to have the tymbre at Kyngeswode heth, and the space to be a fote and halffe betwene the stodes, and he schal have of my Lord for the werkmanschip   14s. 4d.

[July] my Lord paid to a schild of Colchester for 4 cheynes to tey dogges   16d.

1483. September.

Item, for a lok for the saffron gardyn   4d.

[October] Item, for a peyr shoys [shoes] for Tom fole   6d.

William Wastell, harper, for a chylde } Item, my Lord made covenaunte with Willm Wastell, of London, harper, that he shall have the sone of John Colet, of Colchester, harper, for a yere, to teche hym to harpe and to synge, for the whiche techynge my Lord shall geve 13s. 4d. and a gown ; whereof my Lord toke hym in ernest   6s. 8d.

And at the ende of the yere he shall have the remenaunt, and is gown ; and he is bound be endentur to my Lord to performe this covenauntes before wretyn

R. Gyrlynghous collyer. } [December] my Lord payd to Robard Gyrlynghouse, of White Colne, for 10 seme and a combe of collis [coals, charcoal]   4s. 2d.

Whan my Lord went to Colchester for a gret glasse

My Lordes costes at Colchester } The 17 day of Decembre, my Lord went to Colchester, and my Lord came home agen to his dener the 19 day ; and these be the parcelles that my Lord spent while he was there.

Fyrst, in almes to schipmen   4d.

Item, at Noles for a potell of wyne, and a pynt that my Lady had   7½d.

My Lordes rekynynge at Colchester } Item, paid for nedellys and threde 1d. Item, paid to hym that helped in the kechyn   1d.

Item, paid to Tymperleys man for brynging of a hawke   20d.

1484. January.

The lyme makeres sone ⎱ Item, my Lord made covenaunte
  of Colchester ⎰ with the lyme makerys sonne of
                         Colchester, and he hathe promyssed
my Lord to make hym of 20 tone of chalke, my Lord fyndyng
hym hit, and 2 chawder of coles

Item, the 19 day of Jenever, my Lord departed toward London
  to the Parlement. The same day, for my Lords costes at
  Esterford [Kelvedon]   4s. 0½d.

Item, for my Lordes costes at Chemysford, the same nygth
                                        8s. 3d.

Item, for my Lordes costes at Rumford   9s. 5d.

[These are the usual stages of Lord Howard's visits to London.]

1484. April.

John Dyne, the   ⎱ Item, my Lord paied to John Dyne, of
parchemyn maker ⎰ Colchester, perchemyn maker, for 14
                 skynnes velym   4s. 6d.
Whiche stuffe is kytt out for a prykked songe boke for the
  chapell

The Early Life of the Famous Moll Flanders

D. DEFOE : *The History and Misfortunes of the Famous Moll Flanders*,
written in the year 1683

My mother was convicted of felony for a certain petty theft
scarce worth naming, viz. having an opportunity of borrowing
three pieces of fine holland of a certain draper in Cheapside.
The circumstances are too long to repeat, and I have heard
them related so many ways, that I can scarce be certain which is
the right account.

However it was, this they all agree in, that my mother
pleaded her belly, and being found quick with child, she was
respited for about seven months ; in which time having
brought me into the world, and being about again, she was
called down, as they term it, to her former judgment, but obtained the favour of being transported to the plantations, and
left me about half a year old and in bad hands, you may be sure.

This is too near the first hours of my life for me to relate anything of myself but by hearsay ; nor can I give the least account how I was kept alive, other than that, as I have been told some relation of my mother's took me away for a while as a nurse, but at whose expense, or by whose direction, I know nothing of it at all.

The first account that I can recollect, or could ever learn of myself, was that I had wandered among a crew of those people they call gypsies, or Egyptians ; but I believe it was but a very little while that I had been among them, nor can I tell how I came among them, or how I got from them.

It was at Colchester, in Essex, that those people left me, and as my case came to be known, and that I was too young to do any work, being not above three years old, compassion moved the magistrates of the town to order some care to be taken of me, and I became one of their own as much as if I had been born in the place.

In the provision they made for me, it was my good hap to be put to nurse, as they call it, to a woman who was indeed poor but had been in better circumstance, and who had a little school, which she kept to teach children to read and work ; and having, as I have said, lived before in good fashion, she bred up the children she took with a great deal of art, as well with a great deal of care.

I was continued here till I was eight years old, when I was terrified with news that the magistrates (as I think they called them) had ordered that I should go to service. I was able to do but very little service where-ever I was to go, except it was to run of errands and be a drudge to some cook-maid, and this they told me often, which put me into a great fright ; for I had a thorough aversion to going to service, as they call it (that is to be a servant), though I was so young ; and I told my nurse, as we called her, that I believed I could get my living without going to service, if she pleased to let me ; for she had taught me to work with my needle, and spin worsted, which is the chief trade of that city.

I talked to her almost every day of working hard ; and, in short, I did nothing but work and cry all day, which grieved the good, kind woman so much, that at last she began to be concerned for me, for she loved me very well.

48

One day after this, as she came into the room where all we poor children were at work, she sat down just over against me. I was doing something she had set me to ; as I remember. it was marking some shirts which she had taken to make, and after a while she began to talk to me. "Thou foolish child," says she, "thou art always crying" (for I was crying then) ; "prithee, what dost cry for?" "Because they will take me away," says I, "and put me to service, and I can't work housework, and if I can't do it they will beat me, and the maids will beat me to make me do great work, and I am but a little girl and I can't do it" ; and then I cried again till I could not speak any more to her.

This moved my good motherly nurse, so that she from that time resolved I should not go to service yet ; so she bid me not cry, and she would speak to Mr. Mayor, and I should not go to service till I bigger.

Well, this did not satisfy me, for to think of going to service was such a frightful thing to me, that if she had assured me I should not have gone till I was twenty years old, it would have been the same to me ; I should have cried, I believe, all the time, with the very apprehension of it being to be so at last.

When she saw that I was not pacified yet, she began to be angry with me. "And what would you have?" says she ; "dont I tell you that you shall not go to service till you are bigger?" "Ay," says I, "but then I must go at last." "Why, what?" said she ; "is the girl mad? What would you be—a gentlewoman?" "Yes," says I, and cried heartily till I roared out again.

This set the old gentlewoman a-laughing at me, as you may be sure it would. "Well, madam, forsooth," says she, gibing at me, "you would be a gentlewoman ; and pray how will you come to be a gentlewoman? What ! will you do it by your fingers' ends?"

"Yes," says I again, very innocently.

"Why, what can you earn?" says she ; "what can you get at your work?"

"Threepence," said I, "when I spin, and fourpence when I work plain work."

"Alas ! poor gentlewoman," said she again, laughing, "what will that do for thee ?"

"It will keep me," says I, "if you will let me live with you." And this I said in such a poor petitioning tone, that it made the poor woman's heart yearn to me, as she told me afterwards.

"But," says she, "that will not keep you and buy you clothes too ; and who must buy the little gentlewoman clothes ?" says she, and smiled all the while at me.

"I will work harder, then," says I, "and you shall have it all."

"Poor child ! it won't keep you," says she ; "it will hardly keep you in victuals."

"Then I will have no victuals," says I, again very innocently ; "let me but live with you."

"Why, can you live without victuals," says she.

"Yes," again says I, very much like a child, you may be sure, and still cried heartily.

I had no policy in all this ; you may easily see it was all nature ; but it was joined with so much innocence and so much passion that, in short, it set the good motherly creature a-weeping too, and she cried at last as fast as I did, and then took me and led me out of the teaching-room. "Come," says she, "you shan't go to service ; you shall live with me" ; and this pacified me for the present.

"Too Much Poetry, Perhaps"

Colchester in 1800, as seen by VIRGINIA WOOLF, writing of MRS. GILBERT's Autobiography

VIRGINIA WOOLF : *The Common Reader*, 1st Series. 1925

Colchester, about the year 1800, was for the young Taylors "a very Elysium." There were the Strutts, the Hills, the Stapletons : there was poetry, philosophy, engraving. For the young Taylors were brought up to work hard, and if, after a hard day's toil upon their father's pictures, they had slipped round to dine with the Strutts, they had a right to their pleasure. Already they had won prizes in Darton and Harvey's pocket-book.   One of the Strutts knew James Montgomery, and there was talk, at those gay parties, with the Moorish decorations and all the cats—for old Ben Strutt was a bit of a character : did not communicate ; would not let his daughters eat meat, so no wonder they died of consumption—there was talk of printing a joint volume to be called *The Associate Minstrels*, to which James might contribute.   The Stapletons were poetical, too.   Moira and Bithia would wander over the old town wall at Balkerne Hill reading poetry by moonlight. Perhaps there was too much poetry in Colchester in 1800. Looking back in the middle of a prosperous and vigorous life, Ann had lament many broken careers, much unfulfilled promise.   The Stapletons died young, perverted, miserable ; Jacob, with his " dark, scorn-speaking countenance," who had vowed that he would spend the night looking for Ann's lost bracelet in the street, disappeared, " and I last heard of him vegetating among the ruins of Rome—himself too much of a ruin " ; as for the Hills, their fate was worst of all.   To submit to public baptism was flighty, but to marry Captain M. ! Anybody could have warned pretty Fanny Hill against Captain M.   Yet off she drove with him in his fine phaeton.   For years nothing more was heard of her.   Then one night, when the Taylors had moved to Ongar and old Mr. and Mrs. Taylor were sitting over the fire, there came a knock at the door. Mrs. Taylor went down to open it.   But who was this sad shabby-looking woman outside ?   " Oh, don't you remember the Strutts and the Stapletons, and how you warned me against Captain M. ? " cried Fanny Hill, for it was Fanny Hill —poor Fanny Hill, all worn and sunk ; poor Fanny Hill, that used to be so sprightly.   She was living in a lone house not far from the Taylors, forced to drudge for her husband's mistress, for Captain M. had wasted all her fortune, ruined all her life.

Evacuation in 1803

Autobiography of Mrs. Gilbert (formerly Ann Taylor), ed. J. GILBERT
1874

Mrs. Taylor to her daughter Ann.

... On Friday last the principal inhabitants of Colchester

waited on General Craig, the commander here, and received from him the most solemn and decisive warning of our danger, and of the absolute necessity of the female part of the population, with their children, and what effects they could convey, leaving the town with all speed. You will not be surprised to hear that we are all in the utmost distress and consternation. Every face gathers blackness, and our knees smite together. The Rounds are all going to Bath, Lawyer Daniel is packing up all his writings in sacks, and with his family, will send them to Halstead. The East Hill people are flying thicker and faster. And now in this conjecture, what is your advice to us ? Shall we tarry or flee ? and if the latter, pray whither ? Do give us your advice by return of post. You know it is not uncommon to ask advice, and then to take our own ; nor I am sure that to do it *after* we have taken our own is without precedent. Know, then, that this morning our dear Jane, Isaac, Jeff, and Jemima, with a considerable portion of our property, set off in Filcham's waggon for Lavenham. Oh ! could you have seen us yesterday ; the confusion we were in from the top of the house to the bottom, and our feelings so harrowed that we were actually ready to fight one another ! I was up last night to midnight, packing, etc. ; and this morning such a parting ! Oh, how poor Jane did cry ! They are now, poor hearts, on the road, wedged in with chairs, tables, beds, soldiers' wives, etc., etc. May the God of providence watch over them, and bring them safe to their journey's end !

I am not a little alarmed at hearing that should the French land, London will be fortified and close shut up, none coming out or going in ! Pray, run no hazard, but fly if there is the least danger.

Nuts

ROBERT-HOUDIN : *Memoirs*, 1859

[The Frenchman, Robert-Houdin was the Maskelyne and Devant of his day. He came to England in 1849 and, after a season in London, which included two performances before Queen Victoria and the Prince Consort, he went on a provincial tour which included a visit to Colchester.]

It is the custom at Colchester that when a body goes to the theatre he fills his pocket with nuts. These are cracked and eaten during the performance as a species of refreshment. Men and women both suffer from this cracking mania, so that a rolling fire is kept up through the house, often powerful enough to drown the voice.

Nothing affected my nerves so much as this incessant cracking ; my first performance suffered from it, and despite my efforts to master myself, I went through the whole performance in a state of irritation. I consented, however, to perform a second time, but the manager could not induce me to promise a third. Although he assured me that his actors had grown quite accustomed to this strange music, and that even a minor actor might often be seen on the stage calmly cracking a nut while awaiting the reply, I could not stand it any longer, and left the town.

Most assuredly, the theatres in the smaller English towns are not equal to those in the cities.

An Alarming Visitation in 1402

Holinshed's Chronicles, quoted in *E.R.*, vol. vi

On Corpus Christi daie at evensong time, the devill (as was thought) appeared in a towne in Essex called Danburie, entring the church in likenesse of a greie frier behaving himselfe verie outrageouslie, plaieng his parts like a divell indeed so that the parishioners were put in a marvellous great fright. At the same instant, there chanced such a tempest of wind, thunder and lightning, that the highest part of the roofe of that church was blown down, and the chancell was all to shaken, rent, and torne in pieces.

[A pocket-book of the Duke of Monmouth, illegitimate son of Charles II contains this story, copied out in his own handwriting.]

Gout Macabre

T. WHITE : *The Gentleman's Magazine*, 1789

On October 16, 1779, as some workmen were digging a grave in the north aisle of the parish church of Danbury, just beneath a niche in the north wall, wherein is placed the effigy of a man in armour carved in wood, they discovered about thirty inches from the surface of the pavement, beneath a very massy stone, a leaden coffin without any inscription thereon, or any marks where any had been affixed. . . . On raising the lead there was discovered an elm coffin inclosed, about one-fourth of an inch thick, very firm and entire. On removing the lid of this coffin it was found to enclose a shell about three-quarters of an inch thick, which was covered over with a thick cement of a dark-olive colour and of a resinous nature. The lid of this shell being carefully taken off, we were presented with a view of the body, lying in a liquor or pickle, somewhat resembling mushroom catchup, but of a paler complexion, and somewhat thicker consistence. As I never possessed the sense of smelling, and was willing to ascertain the flavour of the liquor, I tasted, and found it to be aromatic, though not very pungent, partaking of the taste of catchup and of the pickle of Spanish olives. The body was tolerably perfect, the flesh everywhere appeared exceedingly white and firm ; the face was of a dark colour, approaching to black ; the throat, which was much lacerated, was of the same colour. The body was covered with a kind of shirt of linen, not unlike Irish cloth of the fineness of what is now usually retailed at three shillings per yard ; a narrow rude antique lace was affixed to the bosom of the shirt ; the stitches were very evident, and attached very strongly.

Feathers, flowers, and herbs in abundance were floating in the liquor, the leaves and stalks of which appeared quite perfect, but totally discoloured.

Whether the legs were crossed or not must for ever remain a doubt, though I am strongly of opinion that they were ; for one of the gentlemen pushing a walking-stick rather briskly from the knees to the ankles, the left foot separated from the leg somewhere about the ankle.

The limbs were of excellent symmetry : the general appearance of the whole body conveyed the idea of hearty youth, not in the least emaciated by sickness. After the above remarks were made the church-doors were opened ; and the parishioners and others having satisfied their curiosity, the shell and wooden coffin were fastened down again, the lead coffin was again soldered, and the whole left, as near as circumstances would admit, *in statu quo*.

Extracts from the Diary of Sir Humphrey Mildmay

H. A. ST. J. MILDMAY : *A Brief Memoir of the Mildmay Family*, 1913
RALPH : *Sir Humphrey Mildmay, Royalist Gentleman*, 1947
BENTLEY : *The Jacobean and Caroline Stage*, 1940

[Sir Humphrey was a member of the Moulsham family of Mildmays, but a Royalist and a much more lovable character than his brothers who are mentioned under Chelmsford. His diary is now in the British Museum and has been quoted from by several authors, but has never been printed in full though the book of Mr. Ralph, an American scholar, is entirely devoted to it.]

4 May, 1634. I went to Lambeth and did swyme at 7 of the clocke.

1 May, 1635. We all went a Maying to Hyde Park to see the Ladyes.

6 May, 1635. At a play this day called the Moor of Venice.

3 November, 1635. To Mr Maine's to supper where I laughed and kissed the wenches exceedingly.

17 March, 1636. I wente to the great dinner of Mr Lathom, reader of the Middle Temple, where was 100 great ones.

2 May, 1636. To my great expense attended my Lord Holland all day at Stratford in the duste.

5 November, 1637. The Morocquo Ambassador shall have his audience this day in all state, I was with my Lady de la Warre there, durty, a foolish sight.

26 November, 1637. A cloudy day and sadd to look upon. I am for the Church God speede me there in his peace. After Evensonge at the wrestlinge, good, very good.

16 August, 1639. My brother [Sir Henry of Wanstead] and his foolish lad came to dinner and remained to this place [Danbury], and saw my bull and dogges play.

11 January, 1640. To Maldon I am going to the Bayley's feaste, there I was and mett with base company and rascally saucy ministers.

12 May, 1641. Heard to the full of the good behaviour of the Earl of Strafforde, who died like a saint to the shame of his enemies.

6 June, 1641. My wife to Graces among the puritans.

7 August, 1641. Soon after dinner my woeman and I did fall out illfavouredly, and so we both continued sullen, till worthily I did acknowledge the error to be mine, when all became well againe and we to supper and bedd.

[Quarrels with his wife were frequent, but short-lived. On one occasion she healed the breach with " two cold pies and a kind letter."]

16 August, 1641. I am going with good company to Goldhanger to eat oysters in coach and troop. The day was hot and dusty, and there we remained all the day and came home in fresco at night late ; to supper and bed in peace.

2 February, 1641. This morning the helly wives of Sandon cut down the rails of their church and burnt them on the green bravely like devils : God send them a day of payment.

9 September, 1641 :—to dinner came Sir Henry Mildmay and

40 with him, well feasted, danced and were merry till night.

17 February, 1642. A rayleinge and lewd letter came to my wife from my brother Anthony by the footboye.

25 October, 1642 :—to Chelmsford in coach to see the foolery and impiety of the Earl of War[wick] and his rabble.

3 November, 1642. Home by newes of the devils abroad plundering.

4 November, 1642. At home all day expecting the Barringtons and plunderers but am safe as yet.

10 November, 1642. Much company here at dinner, all in arms for the rogues.

14 December, 1642 :—timely up the air clear and most sweet, not far abroad but discontented, God helpe me, to dinner and not from home, all day wrangleing with her who has resolved long since not to amende, in peace to supper and bedd.

13 February, 1643. Windy and cold, late in bedd, walking but not far, to dinner, soon after came Jo Griffith drunke, to tavern I wente with him and Parson Vincent, home to sup and bedd in peace.

8 October, 1643. Not to Church, the covenant being hot and I none of the tribe.

[Sir Humphrey later became more and more addicted to " fuddling at a tavern," or as he once writes, " to my ordinary trade of drinking," and seemed equally unaffected by the struggle between the Royalists and Parliamentarians and private losses. On 23 December, 1647, his son Charles died, but on 6 January, 1648, he records, " House full to dinner and no place but music and mirth all the day and night," and the following day : " As the day before less company, and after night to Mother Podd's, the whole family, where we made debauch late."

Another entry in the diary, quoted, without a date, by Mr. Bentley is as follows : "To dynner came Sir Chr. Abdy & went to the newe playe with my wife. I went abroade by my selfe to worse places alone."]

May-Day Carol

Sung by the children of Debden in 1857

BROADWOOD AND FULLER MAITLAND : *English County Songs*, 1893

I been a-rambling all this night,
And some time of this day ;
And now returning back again
I brought you garland gay.

A garland gay I have brought you here,
And at your door I stand,
'Tis nothing but a sprout, but 'tis well budded out,
The work of Our Lord's hand.

So dear, so dear, as Christ loved us,
And for our sins was slain,
Christ bids us turn from wickedness,
And turn to the Lord again.

Why don't you do as we have done,
The very first day of May,
And from my parents I have come,
And would no longer stay.

Of the Beauteous Lady Matilda, and her Murder by Bad King John

WILLIAM VALENS : *Three Ancient and Curious Histories*, 1743

That the Family of *Fitz-Walters* hath of long Time been of honourable Reputation and Account, need not many Proofs.

When *Robert Fitz-Walter*, Lord of *Woodham*, in *Essex*, came to Man's Estate, he betook himself to Marriage, and by his Wife he had one only Daughter, whom he loved most intirely, and caused her to be brought up in Virtue and Learning, wherein she prospered, to the great Contentment and Joy of her Father, and Comfort of her Mother, who, notwithstanding, shortly after Died, and left her sole Governess of her Father's House, which was great. All which she governed, and under her Father ruled, with such discreet and modest Behaviour, as was of all People wondered at, in Respect of her tender Age and Youth. Besides, she was of such excellent and surpassing Beauty, as allured the Eyes of all Sorts of People to gaze and wonder at, Nature having wrought in her Mind and Example of all Womanhood, and in her Body and Countenance, a Pattern and Model of all Perfection ; which, being known at the Court, she was commanded to attend the Court. Being at Court, and daily Attendant on the Queen, the King himself (I mean King *John*) still respecting and Gazing at her exquisite Carriage, and the Perfection of her Beauty, fell so far from himself, and that which became his Person and Estate, that he bent all his Endeavours to solicit her of Love, which she, as fully resolute, most constantly denied. The repulsed King left not so his unlawful Suit, for all her Denial, but practised to procure her Father, to be a Means for his unlawful and ungodly Request : Nature not brooking the Father to become a Pandor to his Child, the poor Virgin, not otherwise able to avoid the importunate suit of this lascivious King, besought her Father, that she might be professed a Nun or Votary at *Dunmow* : Whereunto her Father consented, trusting that her Absence would allay and asswage his Lust, and cause him to leave his unhallowed Suit : But it prevailed not ; but, as a Lion bereft of his Prey, grew more enraged than before ; appointing a Messenger, which he procured and hired of Purpose, whose Errand was, either to persuade her to consent to the King's Request, or by Poison to take away her Life. In the End, when nothing would persuade her, he, accordingly to his Direction, poisoned her. I have read, that it was secretly done with a poached Egg, the Salt being poisoned which was for her Sauce : Others say, with a Cup of Poison, which he enforced her to drink ; But, howsoever, great Mischief befel after this lamentable Tragedy, which well near had overthrown the Kingdom and Country. This was about the Year of our Lord 1213.

Extracts from the Diary of the Reverend Ralph Josselin, 1616–83, Vicar of Earls Colne

Printed by the Camden Society, 1908

1644

Sept. 5. Stung I was with a bee on my nose, I presently plucked out ye sting, & layd on honey, so that my face swelled not ; thus divine providence reaches to the lowest things. Lett not sin oh Lord that dreadful sting bee able to poyson mee.

Sept. 17. My good ffreind Mr. Harlakenden sold one bagge of hops for mee wherin I was advantaged £1 15s. This was Gods good providence.

Dec. 11. Dined at a strange vaine wedding ; a poore man gave curious ribbands to all, gloves to ye women and to the ringers, yett their was very good company.

1645

May 19. Payd 2 yeares tenth to ye Parliamt messenger, £1 14s. 2d. ; ye messenger received from me for his paynes, 3s. ; his power was harsh ; his carriage was yet indifferent curteous, tis a tryall to bee thus dealt withall ; I blesse God my spirit was under, and I hope ever shall.

June 2. At home an alarme, Leicester lost.

June 7. An alarme to raise our regiment of Horse.

June 10, 11, 12. I was out with our regiment ; wee marchd to Walden, mustered, I sung Psalmes, prayd & spake to our souldiers on ye Common at Walden & also at Halsted ; God was good to us in accommadating us and preserving us ; Mr. Josselin of Chelmsford brake his legge at Walden, his horse threw him ; our souldiers resolute, some somewhat dissolute ; the Collonel was pleased to honor me to bee his Comrade ; I shall never forgett his great love and respect.

1646

May 20. This day I had in my garden a full ripe & blowne damask rose : May 17 : the Lords day before, my wife had a fayre bud : I conceived it argued a very early spring.

Dec. 11. The goldsmith of Chelmsford kild & robd up ye

road, as he returned from Braintree markett by three troopers : its Gods mercy and goodness that preserves mee, my house, and that I injoy in a safety.

1647

March 26. [At that time the beginning of a new year.] Our constant loving freind Mrs. Mary [Church] gave my wife a gold ring, and my selfe a silver tooth and eare picke, as a remembrance of her love ; my dearest wife would needs also bee so bounteous as to give mee a silver seale, to use and not loose for her sake.

1648

June 12. On Monday morning the enemy came to Colne, were resisted by our towne men. No part of Essex gave them so much opposicon as wee did ; they plundered us, and mee in particular, of all that was portable, except brasse, pewter, and bedding ; I made away to Coggeshall, and avoyded their scouts through providence ; I praise God for this experiment ; it is not so much to part with any thing as wee suppose, God can give us a contented heart in any condicon, and when our losses may serve to advance Gods glory, wee ought to rejoyce in the spoiling of our goods ; this day I borrowed money for to buy hose, and borrowed a band to wear, having none in my power. I was welcome unto, and pittied by my Lady Honeywood.

Aug. 28. Colchester yeilded ; infinite numbers of people went thither ; ye Councell of warre adjudged 3 to be shott to death. Sir Charles Lucas, Sir George Lile who accordingly suffered, & Sir Barnaby Gascoine an Italian who was spared.

Sept. 10. I drunke my beere for 3 or 4 days with as much content out of a dish as at sometimes out of a silver bowle.

1648/9

Jan. 31. Heard K[ing] C[harles] was executed, but that was uncertaine : he was adjudged to dye Jan. 27, 1648. Bradshaw, the lord president pronounced sentence ; this day was a fast, a very cold day.

ffeb. 18. Great dearth and want of all things, I gave 4*d.* per pound for porke.

1650/1

Feb. 23. This week paste ye Lord was good to us in our

peace, plenty, health, and in the meeting of both sacraments this day, which had not for neare 9 yeares. Wee mett Feb. 20, in a day of humiliacon at the priory, and our God was on our hearts and our company gave themselves to this worke, about 34. After ye ordinance was done, and ye collection for ye poore, ye rest withdrew, wee stayed, & proposed whether any had anything agst another that wee might joyne as one bread ; we gathered for bread & wine, and proceeded Feb. 23 to celebrate ye ordinance.

Wee all sat round and neare ye table ; ye bread was broken not cutt in blessing it, ye Lord poured out a spirit of mourning over Christ crucified on me and most of ye company, and my soule eyed him more than ever, and God was sweete to mee in ye worke.

1652

Dec. 26. I made a gathering for the Indians. I gave £5 and my family, gathered in mony more, £4 8s. 6d. and there was underwritt more £32.

Dec. 30. 52 Heard that ye Londoners bought up bayes, hull [holly] and ivy wonderfully in London, being eagerly sett on their feasts ; oh that my heart were as zealous for God.

1655

Aug. 19. 55 This weeke past God good to mee & mine in many outward mercies ; God left a young hog of mine to be bitten by Burtons dog ; it might have been worse ; they cut his eare & taile & threw him into the water.

Sept. 4. A hog I had died, bit with Burtons mad dog ; blessed be God it was not a child.

1656

Nov. 17. Mrs. Marg. Harlakenden having laid out £120 at London, about her wedding clothes, her father being exceedingly angry, I appeased him, so that though he chid her by letter for her vanitie, yett he paid the scores.

Dec. 15. Mrs. Margaret Harlakenden married Mr. John Eldred ; her father kept the wedding three dayes, with much bounty ; it was an action mixed with pietie and mirth.

Dec. 27. If it bee worth writing this tells that raisins of ye sun were sold at 12, 14, 16, 18d. per pound.

Sept. 3, 1658. Cromwell died, people not much minding it.

Nov. 3.   Sent our squirrel to the Countesse of Oxford, who sent for it, and sent us a silver tankard worth about £3 10s. I esteemed it a merciful providence to us.

1658/9

Feb. 20.   I gathered this day to rebuild a church 11s. 1d. ; oh how lamely charity goeth on such errands, though I prest the worke and exampled it.

1659/60

Jan. 26.   I preacht at Wakes church, snowy, the way bad, twice I slumpt in & was wett.

May 6.   The spring very excellent ; the nacon runneth into the King as Isreal to bring backe David ; Lord make him ye like blessing to our England, and let Gods counsell bee in the worke.

June 10.   A great calme in ye contry.   The Kings proclamacon agst debaucht courses a cutt to the gentry of England ;   oh Lord make him a nursing ffather to thy people.

1660/1

March 10.   This day I heard and then saw the youth openly playing at catt on the green ;   I went up, rowted them ;   their fathers sleeping in the chimny corner ;   Lord heale through grace these disorders.

Ap. 22, 23.   Day to serve the pompous shew, and coronacon at London.

26 March, 1665, Easter day.   12 of us received ye sacrament of ye Lords supper publiquly for which I blesse God ;   I believe its 22 or 23 yeares since received on that day & occasion.

June 25.   Plague increasd to 168.   2063 prisoners Dutch at Colchester [after the battle of Lowestoft].

July 9.   The plague feares the Londoners ; they flie before it & the country feares all trade with London : died 1006 of ye plague 470 : the Lord stay his heavy hand.

Aug. 20.   Londons visitacon sad.   3880 plague, 5319 all diseases.   Colchester seeke into ye country for dwellings.

Oct. 8.   To thy goodnes wee own it with praises that we are preserved from ye smal pox in our town & plague in the country, which is hott at Ipswich, Harwich an 100 dying in 3 weeks ;   at Colchester it spreads exceedingly ;   feares of

Cogshall, Halstead, ffeering.   Certainly at Kelvedon up land, Braintree, and yett Colne, sinfull Colne, spared.

1674

May 12.   Gave Ned Harris 1s. on condicon to be sober quarter of a year & spend only 2d. at a sitting.

1676

Dec. 1.   I cast up my account & I estimate that my mony stocke my debts pd, was about £300.   I thinke I have been to blame in my charitie moneys : straits make us forgett ourselves.   Lord I am now old & I have no worke like serving thee and assuring my salvacon through Christ.

The Lady Mary Defies her Brother, King Edward VI, and Does Not Care for Housekeeping

ELLIS : *Original Letters*, 1st Series, vol. ii

[Robert Rochester, the comptroller, with Mr. Waldegrave and Sir Francis Englefield, two of the officers of the Lady Mary's household, were commanded on 14 August, 1551, by the Lords of the King's Council to proceed to Copt Hall in Essex where she then resided. They were directed to call Her Grace's chaplains before them, and not only to forbid, on their part, the saying of mass, but to prevent any one of the household from presuming to hear mass or any other forbidden rites. They went, it appears, but neglected to execute the chief part of their commission, and refused to proceed on being again directed to execute the charge they had received. The Princess refused to submit to her brother in the question of religion or to agree to another comptroller being appointed in place of Rochester.

Whereupon it was determined that the Lord Chancellor Riche, Mr. Secretary Petre, and Sir Anthony Wingfield, the comptroller of the King's household, should repair together to the Lady Mary's grace with a letter from the King.]

To this her answer was that she would appoint her own officers, and that she had years sufficient for that purpose ; and if we left any such man there she would go out of her gates, for they two would not dwell in one house. And, quoth she, I am sickly, and yet I will not die willingly, but do the best to preserve my life ; but if I shall chance to die, I will protest openly that you of the Council be the causes of my death : you give me fair words but your deeds be always ill towards me.

Finally, when we had gone out of the house, tarrying there for one of her chaplains, the Lady Mary's Grace sent to us to speak with her one word at a window. When we were come into the Court, notwithstanding that we offered to come up to her chamber, she would needs speak out of the window, and prayed us to speak to the Lords of the Council that her comptroller might shortly return. For, said she, since his departing, I take the accounts myself of my expenses, and learned how many loaves of bread be made of a bushel of wheat : and I wis my father and mother never brought me up with baking and brewing. And, to be plain with you, I am weary of my office, and I pray God to send you to do well in your souls and bodies too, for some of you have but weak bodies.

Some of the Misadventures of Mr. Arthur Wilson, the Historian, which he calls "Observations of God's Providence, in the Tract of my Life"

Written by himself

F. PECK : *Desiderata Curiosa*, 1779

1. The 18 of July 1644, hunting in Litley Park, my spotted nag (which afterwards my lord had) being young & not well waigh'd, run away with mee ; &, lepping over a broad ditch, lighted upon a stumpe of a tree, which he flowndring on, overthrew mee & himselfe. When I rose, I could scarce draw my breath. . . . I dranke something to dissolve the putrid blood, & was lett blood in the right arme. But the paine continueth at the writing of this, yet I hope in a decaying condition. For

2. The 21 of July (being the Sunday following) Mr Beadle of Barnston preached at Leeze. His text was, Numbers xxxiii, i, *Theise are the journies of the children of Isreal etc*, insisting upon this. That every Christian ought to keep a record of his owne action & wayes, being full of dangers & hazards ; that God might have the glorie.

3. This made me run backe to the beginnig of my life, assisted by my memory and some small notes ; wherein I have given a true, though a meane deliniation, of eight and forty yeares progresse in the world.

6. And, as I am not superstitious in observing nice vanities, such as the falling of pictures, croaking of ravens, crossing of hares, turning over salts, crowing of hens, & such like simple prodigies ; so I shall not be supercilious for the time to come, to neglect a just acknowledgment of all the acts of God's providence, that all the honor may be given to God.

1647. In November this yeare, holding up a clap-stile in Pond-Parke (where I dwell) for my wife to passe over ; & standing to that end, stradling upon the lower part of it, my feet slipt from the steps, & I fell just upon a pale, some two feet below me, that I satt like one of those souldiers, whose *misdemenors* bring them to feele the sharpnes of the wooden horse. I recovered my feet presentlie ; but almost lost my senses. For, in the fall, the *os sacrum* lighting upon the pale, with my weight there was, for a time, a cessation of the animal faculties. Nature being startled & distorted in her habits, I fell downe, pale & deadlie discolor'd which made my wife cry outt, as if I had beene dying. But after some pause, the obstructed spiritts found their old function ; & I got home : but bruised, and very sore.

1649. The 30 of Julie this year, being at dinner at Leeze, whether some drop or crum, having past the little trap-dore of the wind pipe (which the great Author of Nature hath sett there to prevent such inconvinces) or what other obstruction it was in the breathing passage, I know not ; but I found my breath stopt for a good time ; in so much as they, who sat at dinner with mee, were transported with fear that I was chokt. But it pleased God, after some strugling, to cleare the way, that I might continue yett to be one of those poore creatures whose breath is in their nostrils. Within six dayes after this, hunting a stag in the parke where I dwell, my horse started as I was in full cariere, & run mee under the side of an oak, so soundainlie, that I could not see to avoid a bough which incounter'd with my forehead ; which (had it not been rotten) had knockt out my braines. But it was so wither'd that it snapt in two, & did mee no hurt. Soe constant is the almightie mercie to me ! Which while I breath I will acknowledge. And lett everie thing that hath breath praise the Lord.

Men of Essex Lead the Peasants' Rebellion of 1381

The Anonimal Chronicle of St. Mary's, York, quoted in C. OMAN :
The Great Revolt of 1381. 1906

Because in the year 1380 the subsidies were over lightly
granted at the Parliament of Northampton and because it
seemed to divers Lords and to the Commons that the said
subsidies were not honestly levied, but commonly exacted
from the poor and not from the rich, the Council of the King
ordained certain commissions to make inquiry in every town-
ship how the tax had been levied. Among these commissions
one for Essex was sent to one Thomas Bampton, senechal of a
certain lord, who was regarded in that country as a king or
great magnate for the state that he kept. And before Whit-
suntide he held a court at Brentwood to make inquisition and
showed the commission which had been sent him to raise the
money which was in default, and to inquire how the collectors
had levied the aforesaid subsidy. He had summoned before
him the townships of a neighbouring hundred, and among
these townships was Fobbing, whose people made answer that
they would not pay a penny more, because they already had a
receipt from himself for the aforesaid subsidy. On which the
said Thomas threatened them angrily, and he had with him
two sergeants-at-arms of our Lord the King. And for fear of
his malice the folks of Fobbing took counsel with the folks of
Corringham, and the folks of these two places made levies and
assemblies, and sent messages to the men of Stanford to bid
them rise with them, for their common profit. Then the
people of these three townships came together to the number
of a hundred or more, and with one assent went to the said
Thomas Bampton, and roundly gave him answer that they
would have no traffic with him, nor give him a penny. On
which the said Thomas commanded his sergeants-at-arms to
arrest these folks, and put them in prison. But the commons
made insurrection against him, and would not be arrested, and

went to kill the said Thomas and the said sergeants. On this Thomas fled towards London to the King's Council; but the commons took to the woods, for fear that they had of his malice, and they hid there for some time, till they were almost famished, and afterwards they went from place to place to stir up other people to rise against the lords and great folk of the country. And because of these occurences Sir Robert Belknap, Chief Justice of the King's Bench, was sent into the county, with a commission of Trailbaston, and indictments against divers persons were laid before him, and the folks of the countryside were in such fear that they proposed to abandon their homes. Wherefore the commons rose against him, and came before him, and told him that he was a traitor to the King, and that it was pure malice that he would put them in default, by means of false inquests made before him. And they took him, and made him swear on the Bible that never again would he hold such a session, nor act as a justice in such inquests. And they made him give them a list of the names of all the jurors, and they took all the jurors they could catch, and cut off their heads, and cast their houses to the ground. And the said Sir Robert took his way home without delay. And afterwards the said commons assembled together, to the number of some 50,000, and they went to the manors and townships of those who would not rise with them, and cast their houses to the ground or set fire to them. And at this time they caught three clerks of Thomas Bampton, and cut off their heads, and carried the heads about with them for several days stuck on poles as an example to others. For it was their purpose to slay all lawyers, and all jurors, and all the servants of the King whom they could find. Meanwhile the great lords of that country and other people of substance fled towards London, or to other counties where they might be safe. Then the commons sent divers letters to Kent and Suffolk and Norfolk that they should rise with them, and when they were assembled they went about in many bands doing great mischief in all the countryside.

And the said commons had among themselves a watchword in English, " With whome haldes you ? "; and the answer was, " With kinge Richarde and the true comons," and those who could not or would not so answer were beheaded and put to death.

[All over the county the rebels attacked the officers of the Crown. John Ewell, the Escheator of the county was murdered at Langdon-hills ; at Coggeshall the houses of the Sheriff and of one of the Justices were plundered, at Peldon the house of the Admiral, Edmund de la Mare was overthrown and a bundle of his Admiralty papers stuck on a pitchfork was carried before the local band of rioters when they later marched on London. Special fury was shown in destroying Cressing Temple, the dwelling of Sir Robert Hales, Prior and Treasurer of the Knights Hospitallers and one of the most unpopular men in the realm. Armour, vestments, gold and silver and other goods to a value of £20 were carried away by Ralphe atte Wode of Bradwell and books burned worth twenty marks. In those days lath and plaster houses could be literally " overthrown." In the Paston Letters can be read how Lord Molynes and his men attacked one of the Pastons' houses " with long trees with which they broke up gates and doors " and " mined down the walls of the chambers and cut asunder the posts of the houses, and let them fall.]

Frinton Golf Club

ARNOLD BENNETT : *Journals*, vol. 2, 1932

Sunday, September 28th, 1913

To Marguerite's golf club yesterday. House the most miserable architecture, with no proper place for autos to drive up to, though plenty of autos, and as far as I know, no accommodation for chauffeurs. Whole place too small. Men's room (lords at ease therein) common tea room (devilish cold in winter) and women's quarters. Course beautiful. Shut off from sea by natural sea wall. Some gestures of men playing a ball superb in ease, laxity and strength. Women following a couple of men about who were playing. Doubtless wives or lovers, etc. Immense sense of space. Also sense of a vast organization. But no artistic sense. The architecture I repeat, miserable, piffling mean. And a rotten little 3 cornered flag flying " F.G.C." instead of a superb standard floating in the breeze. The women in white or gay colours were not unattractive in the mass, and some were beautiful, and quite a few pretty. Certain matrons also very agreeable.

The Strange and Wonderful Visions and Predictions
of William Juniper of Gosfield in Essex, Relating
to the Troubles of England, As they were by him
Delivered to Dr. John Gauden then at Bocking and
now Lord Bishop of Exon

From the book of that name, printed 1662

Although I am farre from that vulgar Credulity, or pro-
phetick Itch, to which the Learned Earle of *Northampton*, and
Sir *Francis Bacon*, Lord Viscount Verulam, with others observe,
the *English* humour is very subject, but have rather a regardlesse
diffidence of those Fancifull toyes. . . . Yet having had
opportunity more exactly to know the person, who died
Three or Four years before the happy event verified some of
his late predictions, I think it not amisse by way of diversion
to give even the graver and more serious world (upon the
occasion of my publishing those papers written in the dark-
nesse and horrour of those times) some account of what I
know in those particulars, and with which I was beforehand
acquainted in the worst of Times and Things.

There are two things which give some repute to that that
goes under the notion of *Prophecy* or *Prediction* ; First, the
credit of the Person foretelling ; Secondly, The accomplishment of what was foretold. For the credit of the person,
William Juniper, of *Gosfield*, I know him many years, while I
liv'd at *Bocking* ; he dwelling at *Gosfield* a mile from me, and
oft working at his Trade as a *Bricklayer*, at Squire *Wentworths*
House, the Lord of *Bocking* my next Neighbour ; who would
sometimes tell me merrily, that *Goodman Juniper* had strange
Fancies, Dreams and Visions, but withall that he was a very
honest man.

After some years, now full of trouble and terror, about the
year (as I remember 1649) in the spring time *Juniper* comes,
one morning betimes to my House, very importune to speak
with me ; being told by my servants, that I was not yet risen,

he desired he might have accesse to my Chamber, which I permitted him (looking upon him as a very harmlesse poor man) when he was come to my Chamber dore, he told me (after the usual civility of a good morrow) that he was that nighte commanded to come to me, and to signifie to me that I should Preach, *Holinesse to the Lord, Holinesse to the Lord, Holinesse to the Lord* ; whch he repeated three times with an Emphasis ; & so took his leave ; hastening though a wet morning to go to Four or Five other neighbour Ministers, and sound the same Alarme to them.

This sudden and odd accesse of *Juniper*, confirmed me in the thoughts, that he was a little crazy ; full of Fancies, and more to be pitied, than regarded.

Yet at last hearing from divers hands many strange expressions of his, I sent for him one day, as desirous alone and at leisure to speak with him, to see whether there were any thing extraordinary and remarkable in him.

He very Officiously came in a faire Summers Morning to my house, and walking with him alone in the very pleasant walks of my Garden, I told him, that I had heard many strange things relating to our times, which were Fathered on him ; I seriouly conjured him as in Gods sight to tell me the truth of things ; I told him he could not be ignorant how great a sinne a lye was, especially when forged in a mans own heart and imagination, he should impute it to God, as a Revelation, Vision, or prediction.

The good man (now above Sixty years old) of a very comely and honest aspect, with great plainesse of Speech, gave me thanks for my favour to him ; professed to me that he would not speak any thing but what was represented to him as true ; For Sir, said he, I fear God, to whom I must give account of my words, *etc.*

. . . The War growing hot, and little hope of Peace, (my heart being full of Fears) I had this Dream in the Night ; Passing by such a Neighbours House to a Water-Mill (which he named) and having two little *Beagles* following me (a sport of foot Hunting, which he had sometimes used in his younger dayes) there came out two great Dogs, Full and Fat, which fell upon my Beagles, and worried them exceedingly ; At which I was so moved, that to preserve them, I laid on as hard as I could with this Quarter staffe, (which was now in his hand as he used to walk with it) upon the great Curs, but in vain ; for they were so smooth and fat, that no stroke would fix on them, to make them feel the smart ; upon which I called to the Miller, and asked him, if he were not ashamed to see his great Curs, thus abominably worry my two little Beagles ; he with indifferency, answered, it was no wonder ; for (saith he) my Dogs are called *Will* and *Power* ; upon this answer I was the more *amaz'd*, because I bethought my selfe that my two Beagles were named *Love* and *Obedience*.

I interrupted him, Goodman *Juniper*, would you call any Dogs by those Names of *Love* and *Obedience* : No (Sir) replyed he, God forbid, but in my sleep they were thus presented to me ; as so named ; the *interpretation* be easily made, according as he thought the justice of the *Causes* and *Merits* of the parties would bear. For he was a most Loyall Subject to his King, and a most Religious Sonne of the *Church* of *England*, a lover of Truth and Peace.

"Love and obedience"

Richard I Grants a Charter to " His Jews," 1189

The Royal Letter Book, ed. H. VAN THAL, 1937

RICHARD BY THE GRACE OF GOD KING OF ENGLAND, DUKE OF
NORMANDY AND ACQUITAINE, COUNT OF ANJOU, to the ARCH-
BISHOPS, BISHOPS, ABBOTS, EARLS, BARONS, SHERIFFS, MINISTERS
and all his FAITHFUL SUBJECTS, ENGLISH AND NORMAN, greeting.

Know ye that we have granted and by this our present
charter have confirmed to Ysaac son of Rabbi Joce and his
sons, and their men, all the customs and liberties, as the lord
King Henry our father granted to them and his charter confirmed to the English and Norman Jews, that is to say residence
in our land freely and honourably and all those things held of
us, which the aforesaid Ysaac and his sons held in the time of
King Henry our father, that is to say, Hame [Ham ? East or
West ?], which King Henry our father gave to them for their
service, and Thurroc which the aforesaid Ysaac bought from
the Earl of Ferrers, and all the houses and messuages and
securities which the same Ysaac and his sons had in our land
in the time of King Henry our father.

And if a plea shall arise between a Christian and Ysaac or
any of his children or heirs, he, who shall implead the other
shall have witnesses to prove his plea, that is to say a lawful
Christian and a lawful Jew.

And if the aforenamed Ysaac, or his heirs, or children, shall
have a writ of that plea, the writ shall be for him a witness, and
if the Christian shall have a plea against the aforesaid Jew, let
him be judged by Jews his equals.

And if any of the aforenames Jews shall die, his body shall
not be held back from the earth, but his heirs shall have his
money and his debts, so that he shall not be disturbed ; and it
shall be lawful for the aforesaid Jews to receive and buy all
that shall be brought to them except that which belongs to
the church and blood stained cloth (*de panno sanguiolento*).
Another translation is " garments ").

77

It shall be lawful also for them to go wheresoever they will with all their chattels, as *our proper things*, and no one shall retain them or prohibit them those things.

And we command, that the Jews be quit throughout all England and Normandy of all customs and toll and prisage of wine, as our proper chattels, and we command you and order that you shall keep, defend and maintain them.

Given by the hand of William Longchamp the Chancellor, Bishop of Ely, at Rouen on the 23 day of March in the first year of our reign [1189–90].

[Colchester had a colony of Jews at this time, and in 1191 the following Essex Jews paid tallage : Deulecresse of Berdefeld (Bardfield) £9, less 3s. 4d. ; Benedict, son-in-law of Deulecresse, 4 marks ; Ysaac, master of the boys, 5s. ; David, son-in-law of Deulecreese, 4s. 8d. And in Newport, Mosse owes 10s. from the same. In 1188 Deulecresse, Jew of Finchingfield, brother of Isaac of Colchester, rendered count of 20 marks for waste and incroachments.

See *The Jews of Angevin England*, J. JACOBS, 1893.]

From the Parish Registers

C. F. D. SPERLING, " Some Notes on the Parish Registers of Halstead."
T.E.A.S. (N.S.), vol. 5

Burials

1617. Thomas Harvey commonly called Stammering Tom
       A servant of John Seawell's called Yorksheer.

       Edward Clibberie, seniar, being excommunicated, was
          buried in the highway.   (Son of a former vicar.)

       Thomas Baker called Darling Baker.

1618. John Simeth widower, called Blunt Smith.

1620. A poore girlle that had no feete diing at the almus-
       house.

1639. John Wilson commonly called Ratt.

1641. Thomas Smith son of John Smith, called Stumpps.

       William Gossard had a girle buried . . . 1654, which was
          drownde in a swel tube.

       Robarde Plumbe, he had bine bitten by a made dogs,
          was buried . . . 1656.

1658. Sarah Beadell who lived wickedly and died miserabelly

1666. Thomas Clarke yt was stabbed.

1667. William Rand being shot to death by George Warrin.

1671. A stranger belonging to the monster being drowned by
       misfortin.

Some Other Names

Deaudaty Bragg, 1607.   Repent Savage, 1617.   Lanfrolet
Chicken, 1662.   Malchizedeck Hussick, 1718.   Titus Ves-
pasian Goodif, 1718.   Golden Boosey, 1719.   Pleasance Idle,
1725.

[Although these names are quaint they do not equal those found in
Sussex about this time which included Kill-sin, Small-hope and Fly-
fornication. (*T.E.A.S.*, vol. 2 (O.S.), p. 129.)]

The Bay Loom

[This quotation is part of a poem which was recited at the opening of the Halstead Literary and Mechanics' Institute in 1858, comparing the old Bay and Say Trade with work in Courtauld's Silk Mills.]

w. j. evans : *Old and New Halstead, 1886*

Full well I remember Tom Stammer's Bay Loom,
How it shook with its thumps the four walls of the room ;
How we followed old Tom as he walked up the Lane,
And rode on the log while he " beamed on his chain " ;
A huge oaken log that to one end was tied,
While on it some half-dozen urchins would ride ;
Thus increasing its weight we kept tight every thread,
And the warp round the beam was most evenly laid.
But scenes like this were not destined to last,
And Tom and his Loom became " things of the past."
The days of the Bay Loom still bring to the mind,
Scenes of vice, filth, and ignorance closely combined ;
When the head of the house was too often a sot,
Who sacrificed all to his pipe and his pot ;
His children in rags, without stocking or shoe,
And dirty alike from the top to the toe ;
Their heads like a furze-bush, with thick matted hair,
That shewed horn or bone had but seldom been there ;
Where " Scotch greys " marched on without fear or control,
And took up " headquarters " secure at the poll ;
While " Sepoys " at night, it was painful to see,
Had attacked the " breast-works " of the light infantry.
To these nightly marauders, they " quarter " did give,
And practised the motto of " Live and Let Live."
Then hail ! to the day when the huge old Bay Loom
Was destined, in turn, for the silk to make room,
For the mill and the warehouse have brought to the cot,
Cleanly habits of thrift, which before they had not.

[Further light on the conditions of life in Halstead is given in a. bryant's *Years of Endurance*, quoting from lord rosebery's *Pitt*.]

Toward the end of 1795 Pitt went down to stay with a friend in Essex and, after talking one evening of the good fortune which an industrious and virtuous labourer could enjoy in Britain, was taken by his host to view the dwellings of the poor in the town of Halstead. "The [Prime] Minister" Lord Rosebery has written, "surveyed it in silent wonder, and declared he had no conception that any part of England could present such a spectacle of misery."

[This adds point to the remark of Samuel Courtauld (1793–1881) : "When I die I should like to have written on my tomb, 'He built good cottages.'"]

Harwich Shipping

Lord Howard Sails for Scotland from Harwich with Fifteen Ships, 1481

Household Books of John Duke of Norfolk, ed. COLLIER, 1844
(Lord Howard was created Duke of Norfolk in 1483)

Md. That the 20th yere of the King Edward the iiijth, [1481] and the 23 day of February, I, John lord Howard, endented with the King my Sovrain Lord to do him servisse opon the see, and to be his lieftenant & capteine in the same viage, with 3,000 men, lande men and maryners, wel and suficently arrayed for the werre, for the terme of 16 weekes, toward the parties of Scotlande, or such places as it shal please his Highnes to commande me.

Takyng be the wekke for every man 15*d*. for his wages And for vitels 12½*d*.

The Summa of all this money, wages and vitels, for 16 wekkes for 3,000 men draweth to the summa of } £5,500

Whereof the said Lord Howard hath received be the handes of John Fytzherberd, one of the tellers of the money } £3,528

So is behynde to the said Lord Howard for the wages of his retenu } £1,972

To be payd within this 40 dayes.

[Some of Lord Howard's expenses during the fitting out of the expedition.]

The Brewers at Harwich

The 22 day of Marche my Lord agreed with Claisson, he schal brewe my Lord 20 pipes bere in pipes and barels, that is 12 pipes and 32 barels.   My Lord toke him in hande £4
The same day my Lord is through with Pierces ; he schal brewe my Lord 30 pipes bere in pipes and barels, and my Lord toke him this day upon reknyng   £6.13.4

Item, I, Dalamar, toke my Lord at Harwich chirch   20d.
Item, to a schipman to drynke   4d.

Cobbe of Harwich

The 22 day of March, my Lord solde to Cobbe the boat of the Edward for   53s. 4d.

And my Lord alowed him that he lent Huet 6s. 8d.   Also my Lord allowed him that he had lent to Huet 4s.   And my Lord agreed with him that he schal quyte the anker that is in plegge for 3s. 4d. at Orford.   And also for the goone [gun] 2s.

And also to brenge the maste abowte to the Trigo [one of the ships] from Orwell.   And all this alowed him, my Lord is agreed that he have the bote clere to him selff.

Dalamar

Item, I, Dalamar, toke to them that bare the salt   22d.

The Smythes of Harwich

The 23 day of Marche, my Lord made covenant with Robard Mason and Robard Sporrier, thei schal make my Lord 4,000 calthorpes be Ester next commyng, and 12 for a penny : the same my Lord toke them ernest   13s. 4d.

Thuisday 20 day of Marche, my Lord came to Harwich

Item, a saltfich   6d.
Item, halfe a linge   6d.
Item, salmon   4d.
Item, stokfich   4d.
Item, 24 herenges   4d.
Item, welkes   1d.

Summa 2s. 1d.

Wensday 21 day Marche

Item, a stokfich and half   6d.
Item, 30 hereng   5d.
Item, baken hereng   3d.
Item, hony   1d.
Item, safren   1d.
Item, a saltfich and half   9d.
Item, 2 salt yles [eels]   5d.
Item, samon   7d.

Item, oistres   2d.
Item, oyle   6d.
Item, sinamon   1½d.

[On Thursday, in addition to the usual fish he had :]

Item, oistres   3d.
Item, salt, mustard and venegar   4d.
Item, almondes   4d.
Item, peper   2½d.
Item, figes, rasins and nuts   3d.

[His Lordship was punctilious in keeping his Lenten fast. On Friday the only expenses on food were for fish, figs and fourpennyworth of water.]

The booteswayne of the Mary and the botemen that broght my Lord up and downe
Item, I, Dalamar, toke them be me Lordes commandement 5s.
Item, I toke to persone of Manetry, and to the couper to go
    to Mortemer to seek for houppis [hoops]   8d.
Item, for drynking at Manetry   12d.
Item in almis   1d.
Item, to an ermyte   2d.

[Later entries record gifts of 6s. 8d. and 12d. to " a gentylman, an Ermyte, called Harry, or Hary, Elyse " who may be the same person.]

Item, to the harpers   8d.
Item, to the barbour   6d.
Paid at Harwich to them that warke upon the sayles   20s.
The 25 day of Marche, my Lord toke Brame for the full payment of 8 oxen of one Webbes of Peldon   52s.
For he had received of my Lord afore   £5

[Careful lists were made of the crews and the equipment issued to them, amongst them :]

Buriff, of Brykelsey,
the 28 day of April, my Lord toke him 12 jaketes clothes
                Jamis Atsel, of Kolchester.
He hath a cheff [sheaf] of arowes, a jakete, and anoder for
    Goorge Porter.
                John Eltherton, of Chelmesford.
Item, he hath a peir brigandines
He hath his jaket

84

[Richard Corteman and John Fyeryng also came from Chelmsford, other men from Ardley, Bergholt and Dedham, and several from Colchester and Harwich. Crepage, "Maister of the Trenete of Seint Osis," had a crew of eleven men and received that number of jackets, fifteen bows and a chest of arrows.

The Fleet sailed on 20 May, with Lord Howard in the *Grete Cobham*. Before he embarked lists were made of his requirements :]

Jamis Stoll

Item, in his keping, my Lordes cloth sak, a panyer with spises, the boketes of leder, the almondes, and the rys, the lampreys, and the sturgeon.

To remember the candel.   The mustarde seede.

Item, 3 hoole pieces of arras, 2 carpetes, 2 [cushions] of cremesyn velwet, and anoder of cloth of golde.

To remember the cheesses.

In anoder cofer, 3 peir schitz [sheets] for my Lord, 2 bed-schitz, 10 shertes, 6 napkins, 3 toayles, a bagge with cheste men (silver etc :)

Item, 6 peir hosen.

Item, a long gown of blak satin, lyned with purpil velwet.

Item, 2 doblets of cremesyn satin.

Item, a doblet, popegay colour.

Item, a mantelyn of blewe velwet.

Item, a jaket of cloth of golde.

Item, 2 peir new slippers.

Item, 3 peir other schone.

Item, a long gowne, russet, forred with leopardes.

Harwich Harbour and Shipping

CARLYON HUGHES : *History of Harwich Harbour*, 1939

1388 (Customs Returns)

Christian Arnaldesson imports ermine fells, madder [for dyeing] and herrings. He exports cloth, cheese and peas.

The Cog *Anne* of Harwich leaves with cloth belonging to John Lucas of Manningtree ; and John Bollard and his fellows have wheat in her. Wheat, beans and peas are exported in the Trynitie of Harwich. Wainscot and herrings enter in a Dansk vessel. Giles Pierson imports madder and herrings.

1588 (The Mariners Mirror)

" In these coastes is very great traffique, but chiefly of English clothes, wooll, tinne, pewter, leade, safron, sea coles, firewood and other commodities."

[In 1600 thirty-two ships and hoys were registered at Harwich, ranging from the *Mariegould*, the *Jonas*, the *William* and the *Globe* each of 140 tons to the little *Grace* and the *Burton* of ten tons apiece. Other ships bore such names as the *Christian*, the *Phenex*, the *Delite*, the *Marmaide*, the *Toby*, the *Prosperous* and the *Swanne*. The *Mayflower* of the Pilgrim Fathers was also a Harwich ship. In 1617 copperas, wheat, oats, pease and barley were shipped to London and in 1620 the barke *Kinge*, 120 tons, carried short Suffolk cloths and beer to Elbing.

In the eighteenth century Harwich was the chief port for Holland. In 1711 Sir James Thornhill, the painter, noted :]

" There are in all 5 packet boats, the *Dolphin*, *Eagle*, *Marlborough*, *Dispatch* and *Prince*. The paquets make 20 voyages each in a year. The captain has £10 a month, but by letting his cabin, etc., makes as good advantage as some men of war by ye benefit of victualling his ships."

[The previous year the *Eagle* had been chased by a privateer during her voyage to England. Colonel Harbord wrote to Horatio Walpole :]

" So small hopes remained of escaping Dunkirk that divers gentlemen disposed of their gold to a sort of cormorant damsel who readily swallowed it as fast as we have seen jugglers play with balls. She swallowed 12 Spanish pistoles of one gentleman, and besides what she took in of others, a diamond ring with divers stones of an ancient lady went the same way."

[Colonel Harbord refused such favours for himself and smart seamanship saved the packet from capture.]

All at Harwich

[The arrival of George I at Harwich is commemorated in a saying which was used by Parson Woodforde in 1777, and is still used by at least one old-fashioned East Anglian today.]

" Have been at Harwich that is in a great Hurry all the day long—it took its rise from King George the first landing at Harwich for the first time of his coming to England. Harwich was then nothing but hurry and confusion."

The Diary of a Country Parson, vol. 1, 1924

Victorian Harwich

After the gentlemen had rejoined the ladies, the subject of amusements for the young of both sexes followed. In reply to a question from Miss Archer, Dr. Bremmer said :

" I must admit that, in this respect, the town is singularly deficient ; but if visitors continue to flock in such numbers, as they have done during this summer, we shall very quickly have a troop of caterers for the amusement of the public. Bazaars for the sale of the many pretty little gems found upon our sands and in our cliffs would soon follow. Those beautiful, clear, crystalline pebbles, that make such excellent counterfeit diamonds, will be esteemed for setting, as little remembrances of Harwich. Amber and cornelians might be profitably collected by children, and sold to dealers in these articles. And who knows but it may be thought some day worth while to make models of the Lighthouses, Freston Tower and Wolsey's Gate, at Ipswich, and cast them in cement, all contributing towards a stock of rarities to remind visitors of the interesting places from whence they brought them. To these I may add, that I have seen most beautiful little baskets made from sulphate of copper, the bright blue spars dazzlingly attractive ; and this sulphate abounds here. Then, again there is a quantity of teeth that have been found in antediluvian recrements. I think that, with the aid of a little cement, a variety of ornaments could be made from these. There is a great variety of curious and beautiful geological specimens ; these might be collected and arranged in pasteboard boxes, with glass lids, and, in short, be very like to *Gulliver's Travels*, ' amusing to those who are unlearned in the subject, and valuable to those who are.' Other rarities there are that might well contribute their quota towards stocking a bazaar. Many amusements, suitable to the inhabitants of a select watering-place, would quickly follow in train. An annual regatta we already have."

" Ecstasy of successful election "

During their visit to the Guildhall our party observed several leathern buckets, bearing the arms and names of members of the corporation.

" How very extraordinary," remarked Elizabeth. " What could have been their motive ? "

" It was a custom here, formerly, to exact a bucket from each of the common councilmen," explained the Doctor, " who were admitted to the distinguished honour of being enrolled amongst that body ; and some of them, in the ecstasy of successful election, presented as many as ten ; this practice continued until the stock became overwhelming, when the custom was abandoned, and a sum of money, equivalent to the value of a bucket, substituted."

Barrington Notes and News

Hist. MSS. Com., 7th Report, 1879

[The family of Barrington or Barenton claims to have been settled at the place of that name in Cambridgeshire before the Norman Conquest and Randulfus de Barenton was one of the compilers of the Great Survey, commonly called the Domesday Book. The first written record of their connection with Essex dates from the reign of Henry I, and grants Sir Odynell the keeping of the Forest of Hatfield.

Humphrey Barrington was presented six times in the Court Rolls between 1462 and 1478 for acts of violence : 1 For shooting at Thomas, servant of Thomas Sampson, and saying that he hoped the arrow would go right through his middle ; 2 For an assault on John Noke, the constable, with an open knife called Wode-knyff, when he was fined 12d. ; 3 For assaulting William Benyngton with his lance, fine 2d. ; 4 Striking Roland Wever with a bill-hook, fine 1d. ; 5 For attacking the same Roland with a sword, when there was no fine and Roland was fined for being a common swearer and disturber of the King's peace ; 6 With William White and John Coket for an assault on Walter Bursted with a dagger and knife ; while in 1478 the Court ordered he should not harbour in his house Joan, daughter of John Payn, a woman of scandalous conduct, under a penalty of £10.

By the beginning of the seventeenth century the family were much more respectable and peaceable. A large number of their letters have been preserved from which come the following extracts.]

Mr. Barrington prepares to go to Court

Edward Shaw to Mr. Barrington. London, April 15, 1603.

According to your worship's direction I have enquired concerning the manner of meeting the King, which is generally thought of all to be in black without cutting plain, which divers worthy men of good calling have prepared for, some in black satin and some in velvet, and others some in black stuff. Also much white satin and ash colour and such like colours with much imbrotheringe is prepared against the coronation. Also imbrotheringe is now very dear. Also much gold lace worn, which in my opinion is cheaper and better. There is of divers sorts some trimmed with a small gold lace, and some with a broad, in my opinion broad lace, of either the panes with a cut in the middle is best, nevertheless I would desire you to send me word how you would have it.

[A later Lady Barrington was an aunt of Oliver Cromwell. In 1623 her brother-in-law, Richard Whalley, wrote complaining of his son, Edward, who was later to be a violent republican and regicide.]

O the many harts breaches that this my Sonne brought to your good Sister & the unspeakable sorrowes & cares that he now doth to mee, in that Hee refused my Instructions and scorneth what I say to him. I have in my best fatherly love Remembered to him the whole story of Absolom, & even in particulars. Prayed his consideration & applicacon of that bee to him an ordinnary story. I have named to him of his oune time & of this country 7 or 8 of great accompe, 3 of above 2000 per annum & others of very good Rancke, that have opposed themselves against their Parents, especialle their Mothers, and have consumed their whole Estates even to one foote of ground. 5 of them with much adoe to gett windeinge sheetes, some died under hedges, some allmoste eaten with Lyce & others not able to speake one word at their death. [His son oppresses him for money.] I have atte my Sonne Henries (a good Sonne) a very faire paire of Brasse Andirons & suite of 7 pieces of fyne Tapestry wch I pray you good Sister to buy & send me by this bearer, or the next terme what you please for them, and my Sonne Henrie's sale shall bee as good as if I had sollde them my selfe, for this hard shify my Sonne putts mee to, their souls must answer itt & I wish the 4 to the Phillip : 11, 12, 13, 14. I hope will be prepared as the Appostle saith, and soe good Sister pray for mee & I will bee in this my afflicons & ever

Yor poore & yett not forsaken Brother in the Lord

RYC WHALLEY.

[Lady Barrington's eldest son, Thomas, married as his second wife Judith, widow of Sir George Smith, of Annables, Herts. She was a very strong-minded woman and Sir John Bramston wrote of her as " that impertinent everlasting talker." During his courtship Thomas wrote to his parents :]

I think tis a great advantage to a man to be a successor to a husband not superlatively good. My dearest Mrs. husband was not a fit halfe for her ye worlde knowes well. Yet she ever loved him and he her but what was amiss in him is to her greater commendation.

[*T.E.A.S.* (N.S.), vol. 8.

In 1632 she wrote to her mother-in-law :]

There is much speech of the bravery of a porter that hath taken a brave house and hath his coach and four horses ; the Lord Mayor examined him how he got that wealth, he answered nothing ; then the lords of the Council got out of him that he being the Pope's brother born in Essex, Goodman Long's sons was maintained by him, and tempted much to have come over to him, these two brothers being ship boys to a French pirate, the porter got means to come again into England, but the other being a witty boy was sold to a courtier in Paris, who, travelling to Florence, there bestowed his boy of a great man, who, when he died, took such affection to this boy that changing his name to his own, left his estate to him, and so in time grew a Florentine, a cardinal, and now Pope, and the greatest linguist for the Latin that ever was. P.S. A neighbour of mine in Hertfordshire, one Mrs Kimpton, of some £800 a year, her husband's estate suffered a great disgrace, some fortnight ago in Hide Park, where the Queen as she thought espied one of her gowns that she had lately lost on Mrs Kimpton's back, and so sent to her to know where she had it. She, being out of countenance at such a speech, would not answer, which made it the more suspicious, so that at last she was sent to justice of peace, where she answered also crossly ; but at last the truth was known. The King cried her pardon, would have her brought to kiss the Queen's hands, but she would not, and he offered to knight her husband, but she refused also, but parted fairly ; a poor recompence for so public a disgrace, but the King did nobly in it.

An Example of the Stoutness and Courage of Bishop Aylmer of Mowden Hall

JOHN STRYPE : *The Life and Acts of John Aylmer, Lord Bishop of London in the Reign of Queen Elizabeth*, 1701

All that I have said already sheweth him to have been of a great Stomac. Indeed he had a natural Courage. Which appeared also not in Words only, but sometimes even in Deeds. And now we are fallen upon this Argument, I will not omit a Tradition that goeth in the Family of the *Aylmers*, of the Bishop's stout Heart in a pretty odd Instance. Queen Elizabeth was once so disquieted with the Tooth-ach, that it gave a concern to all the Court. It was in the Month of *December* 1578, when she was so excessively tormented with that Distemper that she had no Intermission Day nor Night, and it forced her to pass whole Nights without taking any Rest : and came to that Extremity, that her Physicians were called in and consulted. These differed among themselves as to the Cause of the Distemper, and what means were properest to be used. There was then an Outlandish Physician of some Note, it seems, for giving ease in this Anguish, whose Name was *John Anthony Fenotus* ; him the Lords of the Council sent for, and required, or rather commanded him to give his Advice in Writing, to procure the Queen ease. Whereupon he wrote a long Latin Letter which I have seen. First, Disabling himself to come after such great Physicians ; and then prescribing divers Remedies. But in case the Tooth were hollow, his Advice then was, that when all was don, it was best to have it drawn out, tho' with the incurring some short Pain. In short, the pulling it out was esteemed by all the safest way ; to which however, the Queen, as was said, was very averse, as afraid of the acute Pain that accompanied it. And now it seem it was that the Bishop of *London* being present, a Man of high Courage, persuaded her that the Pain was not so much, and not at all to be dreaded, and to convince her thereof told her, she should have a sensible Experiment of it in himself, tho' he were an old Man, and had not many Teeth to spare ; and immediately had the Surgeon come and pull out one of his Teeth (perhaps a decayed one) in her Majestie's Presence. Which accordingly was don : and She was hereby encouraged to submit to the Operation her self.

[In 1598 Paul Hentzer in his *Journey into England* commented on the hooked nose and narrow hips of the Queen, and especially her black teeth, adding that this was " a defect the English seem subject to, from their too great use of sugar."]

Margaret, Lady Bryan, Lady Mistress of Prince Edward,
afterwards King Henry VI, to Lord Cromwell, 1538

WOOD : *Letters of Royal and Illustrious Ladies*, vol. 3, 1846

JESUS.

My lord,

According to the king's grace's commandment and yours
I shall accomplish it to the best of my power with such things
as here is to do it withal : which is but very bare for such a
time. The best coat my lord prince's grace hath is tinsel,
and that he shall have on at that time ; he hath never a good
jewel to set in his cap ; howbeit I shall order all things for my
lord's honour the best I can, so as I can trust the king's grace

EDWARD VI AS PRINCE OF WALES, AGED ONE YEAR

Based on the original by **H. Holbein the Younger**. Painted in **1538**
as a New Year's gift to King Henry VIII. Mellon Collection

shall be contented withal ; and also master vice-chamberlain and master cofferer I am sure will do the best diligence that lieth in them in all causes.

My lord, I thank Jesu my lord's grace is in good health and merry, and his grace hath four teeth ; three full out, and the fourth appeareth. And thus fare you well, my own good lord, with as much joy and honour as your noble heart can desire.

From Havering, with the hand of her that is your true beadswoman, and will be during my life.

MARGARET BRYAN.

[It is probable that this letter refers to the painting of the Prince's portrait by Holbein, which must have taken place about this time. The portrait was later given by Queen Elizabeth to Sir Anthony Mildmay of the Chelmsford family ; it is now in the Mellon Collection in America.]

What Shall I Give ?

EDWARD THOMAS : *Collected Poems*

What shall I give my daughter the younger
More than will keep her from cold and hunger ?
I shall not give her anything.
If she shared South Weald and Havering,
Their acres, the two brooks running between,
Paine's Brook and Weald Brook,
With pewit, woodpecker, swan and rook,
She would be richer than the queen
Who once on in a time sat in Havering Bower
Alone, with the shadows, pleasure and power.
She could do no more with Samarcand,
Or the mountains of a mountain land
And its far white house above cottages
Like Venus above the Pleiades.
Her small hands I would not cumber
With so many acres and their lumber,
But leave her Steep and her own world
And her spectacled self with hair uncurled,
Wanting a thousand little things
That time without contentment brings.

95

William Harvey

J. AUBREY : *Brief Lives*

He lies buried in a vault at Hempsted in Essex, which his brother Eliab Harvey built ; he is lapt in lead, and on his breast in great letters

DR. WILLIAM HARVEY.

I was at his funerall, and helpt to carry him into the vault. I remember that Dr Alsop sayd then that he was 80, wanting one ; and that he was the eldest of 9 brethren.

He was always very contemplative, and the first that I heare of that was curious in anatomie in England. He had made dissections of frogges, toades, and a number of other animals, and had curious observations on them, which papers, together with his goods, in his lodgings at Whitehall, were plundered at the beginning of the Rebellion, he being for the king, and with him at Oxon ; but he often sayd that of all the losses he sustained, no greife was so crucifying to him as the losse of these papers, which for love or money he could never retrive or obtaine. When Charles I by reason of the tumults left London, he attended him, and was at the fight of Edge-hill with him ; and during the fight, the Prince and duke of Yorke were committed to his care : he told me that he withdrew with them under a hedge, and tooke out of his pockett a booke and read ; but he had not read very long before a bullet of a great gun grazed on the ground neare him, which made him move his station.

After Oxford was surrendred, which was 24 July 1646, he came to London, and lived with his brother Eliab a rich merchant, who bought, about 1654, Cockaine-house, a noble house, where the Doctor was wont to contemplate on the leads of the house, and had his several stations, in regard of the sun, or wind.

He did delight to be in the darke, and told me he could then best contemplate. He had a house heretofore at Combe in

Surrey, a good aire and prospect, where he had caves made in the earth, in which in summer time he delighted to meditate.

For about 20 yeares before he dyed he took no manner of care about his worldly concernes, but his brother Eliab, who was a very wise and prudent menager, ordered all not only faithfully, but better then he could have donne himselfe.

He was, as all the rest of the brothers, very cholerique ; and in his young days wore a dagger (as the fashion then was, nay I remember my old schoolemaster, old Mr Latimer, at 70, wore a dudgeon, with a knife, and bodkin, as also my old grandfather, which I suppose was the common fashion in their young dayes), but this Dr. would be too apt to draw-out his dagger upon every slight occasion.

He was not tall ; but of the lowest stature, round faced, olivaster complexion ; little eie, round, very black, full of spirit ; his haire was black as a raven, but quite white 20 yeares before he dyed.

I first saw him at Oxford, 1642, after Edgehill fight, but was then too young to be acquainted with so great a Doctor. I remember he came several times to our Coll. [Trinity] to George Bathurst, B.D., who had a hen to hatch egges in his chamber, which they dayly opened to discerne the progress and way of generation.

I have heard him say, that after his booke of the Circulation of the Blood came-out, that he fell mightily in his practize, and that it was believed by the vulgar that he was crack-brained.

He was much and often troubled with the gowte, and his way of cure was thus, he would then sitt with his legges bare, if it were frost, on the leads of Cockaine house, putt them into a payle of water, till he was almost dead with cold, then betake himselfe to his stove, and so 'twas gonne.

The Wisdom of William Harvey
On the Circulation of the Blood

WILLIAM HARVEY : *Anatomical Exercises : De Motu Cordis*, 1628

There is found with us a sort of very little Fish, called in English a Shrimp, and in Low Dutch *een Garneel,* usually taken in the Sea and in the River of Thames, all the body of which is transparent : This little Fish I have often shewn in water to some of my special friends, so that we could clearly discern the motion of the heart in that creature, the outward parts nothing at all obstructing our sight, as if it had been through a window.   In a Hens egg I shewed the first beginning of the Chick, like a little cloud, by putting an egg off which the shell was taken, into water warm and clear, in the midst of which cloud there was a point of blood which did beat, so little, that when it was contracted it disappeared, and vanish'd out of our sight, and in its dilation, shew'd itself again red and small, as the point of a needle ; insomuch as betwixt being seen and not being seen, it did represent a beating, and the beginning of life.

Charles II he enjoyed to his death, and gott seaven thousand pounds, as Sir Christopher Wren told me of, to his owne knowledge. Sir Christopher Wren was his deputie.

His 2d wife, Margaret Brookes, was a very beautifull young lady ; Sir John was ancient and limping. The duke of Yorke fell deepely in love with her, though (I have been morally assured) he never had carnall knowledge of her. This occasioned Sir John's distemper of madnesse, which first appered when he went from London to see the famous free-stone quarries at Portland in Dorset, and when he came within a mile of it, turned back to London again, and did not see it. He went to Hownslowe, and demanded rents of lands he had sold many yeares before ; went to the king, and told him he was the Holy Ghost. But it pleased God that he was cured of his distemper, and writt excellent verses afterwards. His 2d lady had no child ; was poysoned by the hands of the Countess of Rochester with chocolatte.

Christmas at The Hall in the 1860's

M. E. BRADDON : *Lady Audley's Secret*

[The Audley Court of the story can be identified with Ingatestone
Hall. Though the events are of course fictitious the account given
below forms a lively period picture.]

Christmas brought visitors to the rambling old mansion.
A country squire and his fat wife occupied the tapestried chamber, merry girls scampered up and down the long passages,
and young men stared out of the latticed windows watching
for southerly winds and cloudy skies ; there was not an empty
stall in the roomy old stables ; an extempore forge had been
set up in the yard for the shoeing of hunters ; yelping dogs
made the place noisy with their perpetual clamour ; strange
servants horded together on the garret storey ; every little
casement hidden away under some pointed gable, and every
dormer window in the quaint old roof, glimmered upon the
winter's night with its separate taper ; and among other
visitors Mr. Robert Audley came down to Essex, with half-
a-dozen French novels, a case of cigars, and three pounds of
Turkish tobacco in his portmanteau.

The honest young country squires, who talked all breakfast
time of Flying Dutchman fillies and Voltigeur colts ; of
glorious runs of seven hours' hard riding over three counties,
and a midnight homeward ride of thirty miles upon their
covert hacks ; and who ran away from the well-spread table
with their mouths full of cold sirloin to look at that off pastern,
or that sprained fore-arm, or the colt that had come back from
the veterinary surgeon's, set down Mr. Robert Audley,
dawdling over a slice of bread and marmalade, as a person
utterly unworthy of any remark whatsoever.

· · · · · · ·

When Christmas week was over, one by one the country
visitors dropped away from Audley Court. The fat squire
and his wife abandoned the grey tapestried chamber. The
merry girls on the second storey packed, or caused to be

packed, their trunks and imperials, and tumbled gauze ball-dresses were taken home that had been brought fresh to Audley. Blundering old family chariots, with horses whose untrimmed fetlocks told of rougher work than even country roads, were brought round to the broad space before the grim oak door, and ladened with chaotic heaps of womanly luggage. Pretty rosy faces peeped out of the carriage windows to smile the last farewell upon the group at the hall door, as the vehicle rattled and rumbled under the ivied archway. Sir Michael was in request everywhere. Shaking hands with the young sportsmen ; kissing the rosy-cheeked girls ; sometimes even embracing portly matrons who came to thank him for their pleasant visit ; everywhere genial, hospitable, generous, happy, and beloved, the baronet hurried from room to room, from the hall to the stables, from the stables to the court-yard, from the court-yard to the arched gateway, to speed the parting guest.

A Song

Sung by Mr. Pottipher, a shepherd, in 1903

Through bushes and through briars,
Of late I took my way ;
All for to hear the small birds sing,
And the lambs to skip and play.

I overheard my own true love,
Her voice it was so clear,
Long time I have been waiting for
The coming of my dear.

Sometimes I am uneasy,
And troubled in my mind,
Sometimes I think I'll go to my love
And tell to him my mind.

And if I should go to my love,
My love he will say nay :
If I show to him my boldness,
He'll ne'er love me again.

[According to one critic this song has made musical history. When Dr. Vaughan Williams collected it from Mr. Pottipher at Ingrave about 1903 he found in it the catalyst he was seeking for the precipitation of his own style.]

Latchingdon's First Cup of Tea

HENRY LAVER : " More Recollections of By-gone Essex," *Essex Review*,
vol. xvi

My grandfather, John Laver, who lived at Latchingdon, married somewhere about the year 1770, or earlier, a Miss Rush, of Tile Hall, in the same parish. From one of his visits to London during his early married life, he returned with a surprize present for his wife in the shape of a pound of tea, for which I have always understood he paid more than a guinea. His gift also included the necessary equipment for brewing and consuming the tea, namely a set of cups and saucers, a tea-pot, and a tea kettle ; nor did he forget to add a tea-caddy in which to store the costly herb. These I am told, were the first tea-things that my grandparents possessed. The kettle I have often seen ; it was very similar to those still in use in China, and possessed a handle jointed in every part to fall over sideways.

On one occasion when the wife of the groom was about to give birth to a child, my grandmother, as in duty bound, went over to see if she could be of any assistance. When all was safely over she told the women she would like to treat them each to a cup of tea—the new cordial of which they had heard, but had never seen or tasted. The groom was ordered to fill the kettle from the water butt, there being no well upon the farm, which was situated almost entirely upon a belt of London clay. He was gone so long in search of the water that one of the women was despatched to look for him. She found him slowly trying to fill the kettle by the spout from a jug. Never had he beheld such " a queer pot " before, nor had he the slightest notion that the lid was removable. It was certainly the first time that tea was used in Latchingdon parish, but within a few decades " the tea-pond," carefully protected from pollution became an institution at many of the houses.

[Latchingdon and all the Dengie Hundred was very isolated in those days, not only from their geographical position but also from the badness of the roads. Mr. Laver in another article in the *T.E.A.S.*, vol. 5 (N.S.), wrote :]

I have often heard old people say that the roads were so bad that the clergyman of Southminster or Burnham, I am not sure which, sometimes in bad weather did not come to the church for as much as six weeks at a time, and when he did come, would say to the church clerk " after we have finished the service, we will bury those who have died since I was last here " and the two, curate and church clerk, would by the light of a candle in the church porch read the burial service, for the whole, who were already interred.

Master Gerard has a Narrow Escape

Gerard's Herball, ed. JOHNSON, 1633

All the kinds of Tithymales or Spurges are hot and drie almost in the fourth degree, of a sharp and biting qualitie, fretting or consuming. The strongest kinde of Tithymale, and of greatest force is that of the sea.

Some write by report of others, that it inflameth exceedingly, but my selfe speak by experience ; for walking along the sea coast at Lee in Essex, with a Gentleman called Mr. *Rich*, dwelling in the same towne, I tooke but one drop of it into my mouth ; which neverthelesse did so inflame and swell in my throte that I hardly escaped with my life. And in like case was the gentleman, which caused us to take to our horses, and poste for our lives unto the next farme house to drinke some milk to quench the extremitie of our heate, which then ceased.

MORANT's *History of Essex*, vol. 2, 1768

In the reign of Henry III Sewell de la Kerfenere held the hamlet of Cattelegh by finding one ell of Scarlet " ad caligas Regis "—for the King's hose or breeches.

The Parson was given one acre to find a load of pease-straw to litter the church in winter, and one house now a Blacksmith's shop by the roadside going to Braintree was given to buy Bell-ropes.

[No date given for the last item.]

Paying Guests in the Reign of Richard II

H. AVRAY TIPPING : *English Homes*, Period 2, vol. 1, 1929

In 1397 John and Elizabeth Dagaret, of Black Notley brought an action against John, Prior of the Convent of Austinian Canons at Leez, he having ejected them for non-payment of 3s. 4d. They won their case.

They had previously agreed with the Prior that in return for five marks (£3 16s. 6d.) they should have a house and garden within the priory bounds, and a corrody (or daily allowance of food, etc.) in the priory of one white conventual loaf called *miche*, and one loaf of wheat, a flagon of the better conventual ale, two dishes of conventual pottage, one cooked dish of fish or flesh, called " generale," with pittance roast or cooked, and with competent salt. Also fuel and candles.

They were to have a third course on Sundays and superior feasts, and, in Lent, twenty oysters a day.

Parliamentary Elections

[Bramston MSS. unpublished. Though it is not expressly stated that this feast was provided for the electors of Maldon details of it were found among other papers relating to expenses incurred by Thomas Bramston at the County Election of 1734.]

For the Workhouse Treat

1734	By Thos Bramston Esqre.		
Brandy 18 Galls. @ 8/6 pr Gall :	£7	19	4½
Lemmons 34 Dozn Sugar 36 pounds	3	10	0
Wine 6 Gallons	1	19	0
Beer 36 Gallons	1	16	0
Beef 83 lbs @ 4/6		18	6
Ham 18 lb, & Fowls one Dozen	1	1	0
Bread 15 Dozen		15	0
Pepper, Vinegar, Salt, & Pickles		1	6
Butter for Dressing ye Fowls, & Eat @ ye Workhouse, 2 Dishes, & Cheese 1 pound		2	6½
Tobacco & Pipes		4	1
Candles		6	9
Firing		2	9
Glasses Broke 17		4	3
Windows Broke		2	0
Attendants making Punch etc :		5	0
Musick	1	1	0
Cleaning the House		5	0
Bringing & Carring back Forms from Heybridge Hall		1	0
The Servants for Dressing ye Meat, & Washing ye Linnen		5	0
a Candlestick lost, & a Pitcher broke		1	0
Doorkeepers		2	0
	0	2	0
	21	2	9
Himself paid ye Ringers	1	1	0

Dr. Salter, His Diary and Reminiscences, ed. THOMPSON, 1933

I suppose Maldon was one of the most corrupt places in the county, beating even Colchester, which is saying a good deal.

As the time for polling approached, we began to get very down in the mouth, and at one of the meetings we all said Abdy was going to lose—since all the voters coming in from the county were going to be hustled into the public-houses on arrival by six hundred men from Halstead, and there to be kept by liquor and other means from getting to the poll.

Sir Claude de Crespigny was on our committee, and we wondered how to counteract this Halstead move, so Sir Claude volunteered to go to London to get as many prize-fighters as he could, and I was sent to Colchester to get what I could from there. Sir Claude got a company of gentlemen all marked with smallpox, and ready for a row on the slightest provocation. My visit to Colchester realised between two or three hundred, and I stipulated that they should be under captains.

Then the day of the election. I put my awkward squad into The Blue Boar Hotel, gave them some refreshment, and instructed them on no account to go out until they had a written order from me. Up came my Tollesbury blue-jackets in a cavalcade of wagons, and at the tail of each wagon I had two men in command, so that the men should not be induced to get out at the bottom of Maldon's steep hill to be enticed into public-houses. We had an escort on each side of the stopping place, trace-horses were in waiting, and up the hill to vote went my lot of bluejackets.

At the Causeway, going up to Maldon, we were met by Sir Claude's lot, a ragged lot of hungry-looking pugilists.

By noon, all my men had polled and I was standing by Poole's shop when a cart containing men came along with blue favours. The fellows were infuriated, the cart was broken up, the men rolled into the road, and a great fracas began.

Sir Claude's men, seeing the row going on, came down at a sort of canter to take part in it, and you could hear nothing but the thud, thud of the exchanging blows. There was no bad blood there, but the rowdiest election I ever remember proceeded to the end.

We lost by a few votes. The Heybridge Basin men came up at the last and settled it. The Liberals had bought them. They were originally to have had ten shillings down and a pound more if the election was won. Hearing this I suggested 30s. apiece and another 30s. if we won, but we were outbid at the last.

" Excelled Landseer "

Essex Review, vol. iv

Mr. Robert Nightingale, the most distinguished painter of animals, still life, and game of his day, died on the 27th of September (1895) in his eighty-first year. He died in London, but Maldon had been the scene of his life and labours from his early apprenticeship days. Left an orphan at the age of eight years, he was left to the care of two aunts, by whom he was apprenticed to Mr. J. Stannard, painter and decorator, of Maldon. Possibly the handling of pigments, colours and brushes, formulated his innate artistic proclivities, and he soon began to use the colours in the way the power within him led. Young Nightingale soon found out that his nascent powers carried him far away from the mechanical part of his work, and his unassisted efforts in art were a marvel to his companions. His aspirations were so confirmed, and his early success so prominent, that his relatives advanced him the means of attending, as a student, at the class of the Royal Academy, which he entered in 1837.

After so many years have elapsed there is not much information extant as to his early struggles as an artist, but it is certain that he began his early emancipated life by portrait painting, which, in the early days of Daguerreotype, was a separate and recognised profession. In his multifarious work, which included art-teaching, he used to paint public-house signs (including that of the Fox at Rivenhall), ornamental trade-signs, and any general commission that was offered him. In earlier life he was a light well-built figure, and his natural love of horses took him often in to the hunting-field, where he followed the hounds with much enthusiasm, and these proclivities bringing him into familiar intercourse with people of a better class were of great use in advancing him in his profession. He not only painted his patrons' horses, but also their favourite hounds, and occasionally their fat cattle. His fame as an animal painter became well-known and he had commissions to paint some hundreds of horses during his long working life, and notably painted some of the best animals in England for some of the greatest sportsmen of the day. There is no doubt but that his skill in this particular branch became so great as to excel even that of the great Landseer. . . .

For Mr. Chaplin he painted, in life size, "Hermit," the winner of the sensational Derby of 1867, and another sensational picture was Stag, a splendid Arab horse, the favourite of the late Crown Prince Imperial and which he rode at the beginning of the Franco-Prussian war.

Honours List, 1348, after the Battle of Crecy and the Capture of Calais

WROTHESLEY : *Crecy and Calais*, Wm. Salt Arch. Society, 1897

Granted pardon for his good service in the French war.

JOHN HERKSTED of Mauntre, co Essex, for the death of John le Mulnere ; on the testimony of Richard Talbot.

ALEXANDER CLER of Fairsted, on the testimony of Thomas de Ferrers ; pardoned for all homicides, felonies, etc., perpetrated before Sept. 8th last on condition he did not withdraw from the King's service without his permission.

ROBERT DEGHERE of Manningtree also received a general pardon, as did JOHN MAY of Borham and SIMON SPRYNG of Wodeham Walter, on the testimony of Adam de Swynburne, sub-constable of the Army, and others.

WILLIAM DE LA DICH of Wirley received pardon for the death of Nicholas le Arblester, at the request of Thomas de Beauchamp, Earl of Warwick. Dated near Calais, Dec. 24.

[Pardons for murders, etc. were the medieval equivalent of the D.S.O. or M.M.]

Witches' Imps

A Relation of the Examination, and Confessions of the late Witches,
1645

M. HOPKINS : *Discovery of Witches*, 1647

In *March* 1644 [Matthew Hopkins, witch-finder] had some seven or eight of that horrible sect of Witches living in the towne where he lived, a Towne in *Essex* called *Manningtree*, with divers other adjacent Witches of other towns, who every six weeks in the night (being always on the Friday night) had their meeting close by his house, and had their severall solemne sacrifices there offered to the *Devill*, one of which this discoverer heard speaking to her *Imps* one night. The first she called was

1. Holt, who came in like a white kitling.
2. Jamara, who came in like a fat Spaniel without any leggs at all, she said she kept him fat, for she clapt her hand

on her belly, and said he suckt good blood from her body.

3. Vinegar Tom, who was like a long-legg'd Greyhound, with a head like an Oxe, with a long taile and broad eyes, who when the discoverer spoke to, and bade him goe to the place provided for him and his Angels, immediately transformed himself into the shape of a child of foure yeeres old without a head, and gave halfe a dozen turnes about the house, and vanished at the doore.

4. *Sack and Sugar*, like a black Rabbet.

5. Newes, like a Polecat. All these vanished away in a little time. Immediately after this Witch confessed several other Witches, from whom she had her *Imps*, and named divers women, the number of their *Marks*, and *Imps*, and *Imps* names, as *Elemauzer*, *Pyewacket*, *Peckin the Crown*, *Grizzel Greedigut*, *etc.*, which no mortall could invent.

The Examination of *Johan Cooper*, widow, Taken before the said Justices, May 9, 1645.

Died in the   This Examinant saith, that she hath been a witch
Gaole.   about twenty years, and hath three Familiars,
                two like Mouses, and the third like a Frog : The
names of the two like Mouses, are *Jack*, and the other *Prickeare*, and the name of the third like a Frog is *Frog* : And this Examinant saith that shee did send her said Imp *Frog*, to destroy the wife of one *George Parby* of *Much-Holland*, which did kill her within three dayes after.

The Examination of *Anne Cate*, alian *Maidenhead*, of Much-Holland, taken before the said Justices the 9th day of May, 1645.

Executed at   This Examinant saith, that she hath four Fami-
Chelmesford. liars, which shee had from her mother, about
                two and twenty yeeres since ; and the names of
the said Imps are *James*, *Prickyeare Robyn*, and *Sparrow* ; and that three of these Imps are like Mouses, and the fourth like a Sparrow, which she called *Sparrow* : And this Examinant saith, that first of all she sent one of her three Imps like mouses, to nip the knee of one *Robert Freeman*, of *Little-Clacton*, whom the said Imp did so lame, that the said *Robert* dyed on that lamenesse within half a yeere after : And this Examinent

saith, that she sent her said Imp *Sparrow*, to kill the child of one *George Parby* of *Much-Holland*, which child the said Imp did presently kill ; and that the offence this Examinant took against the said *George Parby* to kill his said childe, was, because the wife of the said *Parby* denyed to give this Examinant a pint of Milke : And this Examinant further saith, that shee sent her said Imp *Sparrow* to the house of *Samuel Ray*, which in a very short time did kill the wife of the said *Samuel* : and that the cause of this Examinants malice against the said woman was, because shee refused to pay to this Examinant two pence which she challenged to be due to her ; And that afterwards her said Imp *Sparrow* killed the said child of the said *Samuel Ray*.

The testimony of Sir *Thomas Bowes*, Knight, which he *spake upon the Bench, concerning the aforesaid* Anne West, *shee being then at the Barre upon her tryall*.

That a very honest man of *Manningtree*, whom he knew would not speak an untruth, affirmed unto him, that very early one morning, as he passed by the said *Anne Wests* dore, perceiving her dore to be open, looked into the house, and presently there came three or foure little things in the shape of black rabbits, leaping and skipping about him, who having a good stick in his hand, struck at them, thinking to kill them, but could not, but at last caught one of them in his hand, and holding it by the body of it, he beat the head of it against his stick, intending to beat out the braines of it ; but when he could not kill it that way, he tooke the body of it in one hand, and the head of it in another, and indeavoured to wring off the head ; and as he wrung and stretched the neck of it, it came out between his hands like a lock of wooll ; yet he would not give over his intended purpose, but knowing a Spring not farre off, he went to drowne it ; but still as he went he fell downe, and could not goe but downe he fell againe, so that he at last crept upon his hands and knees till he came at the water, and holding it fast in his hand, he put his hand downe into the water up to his elbow, and held it under water a good space, till he conceived it was drowned, and then letting goe his hand, it sprung out of the water up into the aire, and so vanished away.

A Wandering Musician

Essex County Sessions Rolls, Hist. MSS. Com., 10th Report

14. Elizabeth (1572). A Petition of divers undersigned persons (in favour of George Writt, musician) to the Justices of the Peace of Essex, praying that the said George Writt may have license to follow his calling : " To all true Christian people to whom this present writinge shall come to be sene, rede or hard, George Writt, Tayler and muzison, inhabiting in Maplestead Magna in the countye of Essex, being a pore man, having a wyfe & fyve children & twoe prentices, laboring for his living with these towe sciences as an honest man ought to do, And whereas the foresaid George Writt was wont to travell the countrye with his instrumentes to Brydhales [Bridals] & to other places, being thereunto required, & using him selfe in good order according to honestie and truthe, Whereas yt is nowe sett for the by the Lawes of this realme, . . . That none shall travell without Licenc granted out by the honorable & Worshipeful of this realme, The Quenes Maiesties Justices, Wherfore we would desire your favour to grant vnto this poore man licence, that he maye travell the countrye & mayntayne his pore living according to the Lawes of this realme. . . . Geven the vi daye of September, Ao. Dni. 1572. By us—

John Holinshed, gent., Willm. Martin," and eight others.

EDWARD THOMAS : *Collected Poems*

*If I were to own the countryside
As far as a man in a day could ride,
And the Tyes were mine for giving or letting—
Wingle Tye and Margaretting
Tye—and Skreens, Gooshays, and Cockerells,
Shellow, Rochetts, Bandish, and Pickerells,
Martins, Lambkins, and Lillyputs,
Their copses, ponds, roads, and ruts,
Fields where plough-horses steam and plovers
Fling and whimper, hedges that lovers
Love, and orchards, shrubberies, walls
Where the sun untroubled by north wind falls,
And single trees where the thrush sings well
His proverbs untranslatable,
I would give them all to my son
If he would let me any one
For a song, a blackbird's song, at dawn.
He should have no more, till on my lawn
Never one was left, because I
Had shot them to put them into a pie—
His Essex blackbirds, every one,
And I was left old and alone.*

*Then unless I could pay, for rent, a song
As sweet as a blackbird's, and as long—
No more—he should have the house, not I ;
Margaretting or Wingle Tye,
Or it might be Skreens, Gooshays, or Cockerells,
Shellow, Rochetts, Bandish, or Pickerells,
Martins, Lambkins, or Lillyputs,
Should be his till the cart tracks had no ruts.*

" Love . . . is an Ever-fixed Mark "

Mr. Luckyn, afterwards Sir Capell Luckyn, writes to his wife, Mary,
daughter of Sir Harbottle Grimston

[They had been married in 1647 when he was 25 years old and she
15. As will be seen below Messing was bought for the young couple
in 1650.]

T.E.A.S., vol. 6 (N.S.)

Dearest Heart

I can not but imbrace all oppertunitys to congratulate thee,
& to let thee heare of my welfare wch I am confident thou
rejoyces to heare of. Such as thy poore servant can furnish
you with cordially he presents you wth twoe of ye best piggs
that are at this tyme in ye parish & I believe if he had any
thing better you might commande it.

. . . Pray keape yourselfe warme & gitt rid of your Cough
least when I come I finde both you & your Mayde both guilty
of the breach of my Directions wch was to keape yor selfe
wormer & free from all cold. . . .

Thy ever constant Husband

C. LUCKYN

Hutton, 25 Decem. 1648.

Sweatest Heart.

. . . Be please my (dearest) to accept of, what thy poore
country Orchard of Hutton can afford, wch is a Basket of
wardens [pears] to the number of a pecke the worst are at the
tope because they shold give noe incoragement to any that
had a mind to steale the whole : Did I know any thing heare
worth the sending to thee I wold either send it or bring it my
selfe, in the interim accept of this scribled paper, assuring the
that I my selfe am hasning to the wth all spead that may bee.
I am

Thy ever loving and constant Husband

C. LUCKYN.

Hutton, 16th of October 1649.

My only Joy

My heart thursteth after thy Company, & weare it in my power I should be sooner wth thee then this paper can express. . . . My Lady was buried on Saturday night, after we came to Bradfeild, none attending on her corpes, but her owne family, saving Mr Goody, who pretended he came thither rather by chance, then any thing else, he went away from Bradfeild on Munday morning. As soone as he was gone (we) went into my Ladyse Chamber, to search for her will . . . she has given the Cabinet wch your Mother gave her, and a booke wch My Lady Covintry gave her. For other perticulers, I shall acquainte you wth when I shall have the happyness to kisse yor faier hande. As thou loves me, have a care of thy selfe and let Besse know I shall thinke of her, as she has care of thee, & if I find thou hast taken cold, I shall wholy impute it to her carlessnesse of thee. . . .

Bradfeild, 12th of December, 1649.

Sweetest Heart :

Though absent yet thus farre happy, that I dayly see your picture which is in your Fathers Chamber ; it puts me in minde of you if I had nothing else but that to thinke of but your other vertues & good disposition wth the future hopes of your and my sonne shall hasten me to see you as soone as possible I can. . . . I have sent you the Handkerchers they are the best Mrs. Constable has if you dislike anything she will change it. I bought the Cappes, Handkerchers & gloves of her ; so for the child coets, if you dislike, return them. My sweetest if they not soe as thou deserves & and I wish, it is my fault of skill and not [of] will to please you. I present you with a small present twoe Cornelian Rings I wish them better for thy sake if they doe not fit I can change them if you let me know what Bignesse you will have them. My Dearest be assured I shall to my utmost supplicate the Lord for a blessing uppon you and your Little one. For gods sake have a care you git noe colde but have a great care of yourselfe, and you shall ever oblige

Yor ever constant & loving Husband

Friday the 25th of October 1650   C. LUCKYN.

My only Joy

There is nothing soe joyfull to me, as the assurance of thine and the Babes good health. I pray god stil to continue to you and me that good tydings. I thanke thee that thou art so well please with the commodities which I have bought and sent thee downe by Woodward. I shall be very glad that by your next oppertunitie you would favor me so farre as to acquainte me with your resolution what gowne you would have for the winter, and whither you hold your resolution to have it in the Country or from Stockwells. I pray you let it be very warme . . . I praise god althings are likely to goe on well, there is a very good understanding betwixt your Father and my Father. By my next you will heare that Messin is settle upon you, and that Hutton is solde. Your Father orders all, we are like to have sixe thousand five hundred powndes for Hutton, your Father gives us three hundred powndes and my Father besides the five hundred powndes will settle Saint Osith uppon you wholly. Be you sure to give your Father thankes in your next letter to him for £300 wch he gives you. This good news will not please my Lady Luckyn who is in the Country so I am in hopes we shall be settle in Messin and run not one penny more in debt. . . .

The first of November 1650.

Most Beloved Hearte

I thanke thee that thou art please to take notice of that affection, wch I desired to demonstrate to you though uppon the roade by John Townsend : if I had met with him any where but a myle from a house, I should have written to you, though much more a blotted letter then now this is. . . . For your Comfert I have been at Messin I like [it] farre better than Hutton it is an Anchient house fitter for a Gentleman to live in & good growne. I am

     Thy ever loving & Constant husband

        C. LUCKYN.

1st Feb. 1651. Lyncolnes Inne

William Newman, one of the King's Trumpets, to Lord Lisle, Deputy of Calais, 6 February, 1535

Letters and Papers of Henry VIII, ed. GAIRDNER, vols. 8 and 10, 1885

I beg you to help a brother-in-law of mine Thomas Layer, of Owvyngton, Essex, yeoman, to a warrant for a protection, " by the same token that your Lordship took me by the hand through the grate at the Lantern gate at my last being with you, and moreover, by the same token I sent you a dog by the ferrar of the town, which dog's name is Wolf ; and I heartily thank your Lordship for my dog you gave me."

(The protection was granted, as requested, to Thos. Layer, of Ovington, yeoman, going in the retinue of Sir Arthur Plantagenet, viscount Lisle, deputy-general of Calais. Feb. 14, 1536.)

The Essex Chronicle, 1919

P.-c. Cook joined the Essex Constabulary in 1888. The most sensational episode of his career occurred over 20 years ago at Pebmarsh. He was called one morning to a farm where a madman had murdered another man by cutting off his head. He found the murderer in a state of frenzy, walking about with his victim's head in a bowl under one arm and with two dead chickens and a gun in the other hand.

The Castle of Pleshey

NICHOLS : *Royal Wills*, 1780

Humphrey de Bohun, Earl of Hereford and Essex, died, unmarried, at Pleshey 1361. He bequeathed :—

To our dear nephew Humfray de Bohun a noche, or gold stud, surrounded by large pearls with a ruby . . . to Elizabeth our niece of Northampton, our bed with the arms of England . . . to our niece dame Katerine Dengayn £40 for her chamber. To our sister Countess of Devonshire our green bed powdered with vermilion roses with all its apparel, and a chapelet gobonne with large sapphires and large pearls, and a bacyn darrein, in which we were accustomed to wash our head, and which belonged to Madame my mother.

The Arrest and Murder of Thomas of Woodstock, Duke of Gloucester, by his nephew Richard II

Froissart's Chronicles, Lord Berner's translation

On a day the king in maner as goyng a huntynge he rode from Haverynge of Boure a xx myle from London in Essex and within xx myle of Plashey where the duke of Gloucester helde his house. After dyner, the kinge departed from Havering with a small company, and came to Plashey about v a clocke ; the weder was fayre and hote. So the kyng came sodainly thyder about the tyme that the duke of Gloucester had supped, for he was a small eater nor sat never long at dyner nor at supper. When he herde of the kinge's comynge he went to meet hym in the myddel of the court, and so did the duchesse and her chyldren, and they welcomed the kyng, and the kyng entered into the hall and so into a chambre. Than a borde was spredde for the kynge's supper. The kynge satte not longe, and sayd at his fyrst cominge, " Faire uncle, cause fyve or six horses of yours to be sadylled, for I wyll praye you to ryde with me to London, as tomorrowe the

Londoners wyll be before us. And there wyll be also myne uncles of Lancastre and Yorke with dyvers other noblemen. For upon the Londoners requestes I wyll be ordred accordyng to your counsayle, and commaunde your stewarde to follow you with your trayne to London, where they shall fynde you." The duke, who thought none yvell, lightly agreed to the kynge. And whan the kynge had supped and rysen, every thynge was ready. The kynge than toke leave of the duchesse and of her children, and lepte a horsebacke, and the duke with hym, accompanyed all onely but with sevyn servauntes, thre squyers, and foure yeomen, and tooke the waye of Bondelay, to take the playne waye and to eshewe Brendwode and London commen hyghewaye. So they rode a greet payce, and talked by the way with his uncle, and he with hym, and so aproched to Stratforde on the ryver of Thames. When the kyng came nere to the bushment that he had layde, than he rode from his uncle a great pace, and lefye hym somewhat behynde hym. Than sodaynly the erle-marshall with his bande came galopyng after the duke, and overtoke hym, and saide, " Sir, I arest you in the kynge's name." The duke was abashed with that worde, and sawe well he was betrayed, and began to call loude after the kynge. I can nat tell wheder the kyng herde hym or nat, but he turned nat, but rode forthe rather faster than he dyde before.

A Further Account in a MS. Chronicle

Quoted in GOUGH : *A History of Pleshey*, 1803

And than after this the kynge for pure malys that he had agenst his uncle the duc of Glouc' and therl of Arundell and therl of Warr' thrugh fals counsaille he rode that same tyme into Essex with a gret strength unto Chelmesford, and so to Plashye sodenly to Sir Thomas of Wodstoke the gode duc of Gloucester, and arrested hym, and he was ladde down to the water, and put into a shippe, and [*anon*] had hym to Calais into the captane's warde, there to be surely kept by the king's comaundement, and [*anon*] after this the captayne was comaunded to put hym to deth, and than the kepers toke her counsaill hough thei myght put hym to dethe. So thei come upon hym in his bedde whan he was on slepe, and smored hym thus. Thei toke two smalle towels, and made of hem ij rydyng knotts, and kaste them abote the duks nek, and toke a federbed, and laid it upon hym, and some ley upon the ffederbed, and some drughe the towels unto the tyme he were dede, and thus thei strangled this noble duc on whose soule God have mercy, Amen.

Rivers and Revenge

WILLIAM HARRISON, Rector of Radwinter and Canon of Windsor :
Description of England, 1587

There is a pretie water that beginneth neere unto Gwinbach
or Winbeche church in Essex, a towne of old, and yet belonging to the Fitzwaters, taking name of Gwin, which is beautifull
or faire, & Bache that signifieth a wood : and not without
cause, sith not onlie the hilles on ech side of the said rillet,
but the whole paroch hath sometime abounded in woods.
This said brooke runneth directlie from thence unto Radwinter. By the waie also it is increased with sundrie pretie
springs, of which Pantwell is the cheefe and which (to saie
the truth) hath manie a leasing fathered on the same. Certes
by the report of common fame it hath beene a pretie water,
and of such quantitie, that botes have come in times past from
Bilie abbeie beside Maldon unto the mores in Radwinter for
corne. I have heard also that an anchor was found there
neere to a red willow, when the water-courses by act of parlement were survied and reformed throughout England, which
maketh not a little with the aforesaid relation. But this is
strangest of all, that a lord sometime of Winbech (surnamed
the great eater, because he would breake his fast with a whole
calfe, and find no bones therein, as the fable goeth) falling at
contention with the lord John of Radwinter, could worke
him none other injurie, but by stopping up the head of Pantwell, to put by the use of a mill which stood by the church of
Radwinter, and was served by that brooke abundantlie.
Certes I know the place where the mill stood, and some posts
thereof do yet remaine. But see the malice of mankind,
wherebey one becommeth a woolfe unto the other in their
mischeevuous moodes. For when the lord saw his mill to be
so spoiled, he in revenge of his losse, brake the necke of his
adversarie, when he was going to horsebacke, as the constant
report affirmeth. For the lord of Radwinter holding a
parcell of his manour of Radwinter hall of the Fitzwaters, his

sonne was to hold his stirrop at certeine times when he should demand the same. Shewing himselfe therefore prest on a time to doo his said seruice, as the Fitzwater was readie to lift his leg ouer the saddle, he by putting backe his foot, gaue him such a thrust that he fell backward, and brake his necke : wherevpon insued great trouble, till the matter was taken vp by publike authoritie : and that seruile office conuerted into a pound of pepper, which is truelie paid to this daie.

"neere to a red willow"

Anne Boleyn and King Henry VIII

WOOD : *Letters of Royal and Illustrious Ladies*, vol. 2, 1846

[The whereabouts of the original letter is unknown ; this is a re-translation from an Italian translation in *Leli*, Vita de Elisabetha. The date is also unknown but it was probably written about 1519 when Anne Boleyn received her appointment as Maid of Honour to Queen Catherine.

Rochford Hall belonged to Anne's father and is traditionally the place of her birth ; her brother was created Viscount Rochford about 1530.]

SIRE :

It belongs only to the august mind of a great king, to whom Nature has given a heart full of generosity towards the sex, to repay by favours so extraordinary an artless and short conversation with a girl. Inexhaustable as is the treasury of your majesty's bounties, I pray to consider that it cannot be sufficient to your generosity ; for if you recompense so slight a conversation by gifts so great, what will you be able to do for those who are ready to consecrate their entire obedience to your desires ? How great soever may be the bounties I have received, the joy that I feel in being loved by a king whom I adore, and to whom I would with pleasure make a sacrifice of my heart, if fortune had rendered it worthy of being offered to him, will ever be infinitely greater.

The warrant of maid of honour to the queen induces me to think that your majesty has some regard for me, since it gives me the means of seeing you oftener, and of assuring you by my own lips (which I shall do on the very first opportunity) that I am,

Your Majesty's very obliged and very obedient servant, without any reserve,   ANNE BOLEYN.

The King Pleads with Anne

[This and the following letter, two of seventeen, are now in the Vatican Library at Rome. They are in French and undated and have only recently been published in accurate copies in *The Love Letters of Henry VIII*, ed. SAVAGE, 1949, though they have been known and printed for over 100 years.]

In debating with myself the contents of your letters I have been put to a great agony ; not knowing how to understand them, whether to my disadvantage as shown in some places, or to my advantage as in others. I beseech you now with all my heart definitely to let me know your whole mind as to the love between us ; for necessity compels me to plague you for a reply, having been for more than a year now struck by the dart of love, and being uncertain either of failure or of finding a place in your heart and affection, which point has certainly kept me for some time from naming you my mistress, since if you love me with an ordinary love the name is not appropriate to you (. . .) but if it pleases you to do the duty of a true, loyal mistress and friend, and to give yourself body and heart to me, who have been and will be, your very loyal servant (if your rigour does not forbid me), I promise you that not only the name will be due to you, but also to take you as my sole mistress, casting off all others than yourself out of my mind and affection, and to serve you only ; begging you to make a complete reply to this my rude letter as to how far and in what I can trust ; and if it does not please you to reply in writing, to let me know of some place where I can have it by word of mouth, the which place I will seek out with all my heart. No more for fear of wearying you. Written by the hand of him who would willingly remain your

H. R.

The reasonable request of your last letter with the pleasure also that I take to know them true causeth me to send you now these news : the legate which we most desired arrived at Paris on Sunday or Monday last past so that I trust by the next Monday to hear of his arrival at Calais [with the divorce from Catherine] and then I trust within a while after to enjoy that which I have so long longed for to God's pleasure and our both comfort ; no more to you at this present mine own darling for lack of time, but that I would that you were in my arms or I in yours, for I think it long since I kissed you ;

written after the killing of an hart at 11 of the clock, minding with God's grace tomorrow mightily timely to kill another ; by the hand of him which I trust shortly shall be yours.

HENRY R.

The End of the Story : the Execution of Anne, and of her Brother Viscount Rochford in May 1536

Letters and Papers of Henry VIII, vol. 10, Vienna Archives

The count Rochefort, was beheaded with an axe upon a scaffold before the Tower of London (on May 17th). He made a very catholic address to the people, saying he had not come hither to preach, but to serve as a mirror and example, acknowledging his sins against God and the King. . . .

The said queen (unjustly called) finally was beheaded upon a scaffold within the Tower with open gates (on May 19th). She was brought by the captain upon the said scaffold, and four young ladies followed her. She looked frequently behind her, and when she got upon the scaffold was very much exhausted and amazed. She begged leave to speak to the people, promising to say nothing but what was good. The captain gave her leave, and she began to raise her eyes to Heaven, and cry mercy to God and to the King for the offence she had done, desiring the people always to pray to God for the King, for he was a good, gentle, gracious, and aimable prince. She was then stripped of her short mantle furred with ermines, and afterwards took off her hood, which was of English make, herself. A young lady presented her with a linen cap, with which she covered her hair, and she knelt down, fastening her clothes about her feet, and one of the ladies bandaged her eyes.

Immediately the executioner did his office ; and when her head was off it was taken by a young lady and covered with a white cloth. Afterwards the body was taken by the other ladies, and the whole carried into the church nearest the Tower of London. It was said that she was condemned to be burnt alive, but that the King commuted her sentence to decapitation. Thus, he who wrote this billet says that, according to the old writings, he has seen the prophecy of Merlin fulfilled.

Match Making at Dagnams, the Seat of Lady Wright, Sister of Lady Sandwich

The Diary of Samuel Pepys, vol. 5, ed. WHEATLEY, 1900

1665. July 14th. In the evening, I by water to Sir G. Carteret's, and there find my Lady Sandwich and her buying things for my Lady Jem's wedding ; and my Lady Jem. is beyond expectation come to Dagenhams, where Mr Carteret is to go visit her tomorrow ; and my proposal of waiting on him, he being to go alone to all persons strangers to him, was well accepted, and so I go with him. But, Lord ! to see how kind my Lady Carteret is to her ! Sends her most rich jewells, and provides bedding and all things of all sorts most richly for her, which makes my Lady and me out of our wits almost to see the kindnesse she treats us all with, as if they would buy the young lady.

15th. Up, and after all business done, though late, I to Deptford, and after dinner, at Sir G. Carteret's, and anon took boat, Mr Carteret and I to the ferry-place at Greenwich, and there staid an hour crossing the water to and again to get our coach and horses over ; and by and by set out, and so toward Dagenhams. But, Lord ! what silly discourse we had by the way as to love-matters, he being the most awkerd man I ever met with in my life as to that business. Thither we come, by that time it begun to be dark, and were kindly received by Lady Wright and my Lord Crew. And to discourse they went, my Lord discoursing with him, asking of him questions of travell, which he answered well enough in a few words, but nothing to the lady from him at all. To supper, and after supper to talk again, he yet taking no notice of the lady. My Lord would have had me have consented to leaving the young people together to-night, to begin their amours, his staying being but to be little. But I advised against it, lest the lady might be too much surprised. So they led him up to his chamber, where I said a little, to know how he liked the lady, which he told me he did mightily ; but, Lord ! in the dullest insipid manner that ever lover did. So I bid him good night, and down to prayers with my Lord Crew's family, and after prayers, my Lord, and Lady Wright, and I to consult what to do ; and it was agreed at last to have them go to church together, as the family used to do, though his lameness was a great objection against it. But at last my Lady Jem. sent me word by my Lady Wright that it would be better to do just as they used to do before his coming ; and therefore she desired to go to church, which was yielded then to.

16th (Lord's day). I up, having lain with Mr. Moore in the chaplin's chamber. And having trimmed myself, down to Mr. Carteret ; and he being ready we down and walked in the gallery an hour or two, it being a most noble and pretty house that ever, for the bigness, I saw. Here I taught him what to do : to take the lady always by the hand to lead her, and telling him that I would find opportunity to leave them two together, he should make these and these compliments, and also take a time to do the like to Lord Crew and Lady Wright. After I had instructed him, which he thanked me for, owning that he needed my teaching him, my Lord Crew come down and family, the young lady among the rest ; and so by coaches to church four miles off ; where a pretty good sermon, and a declaration of penitence of a man that had undergone the Churche's censure for his wicked life. Thence back again by coach, Mr. Carteret having not had the confidence to take his lady once by the hand, coming or going, which I told him of when we come home, and he will here-after do it. So to dinner. My Lord excellent discourse. Then to walk in the gallery, and to sit down. By and by my Lady Wright and I go out (and then my Lord Crew, he not by design), and lastly my Lady Crew come out, and left the young people together. And a little pretty daughter of my Lady Wright's most innocently come out afterward, and shut the door to, as if she had done it, poor child, by inspiration ; which made us without, have good sport to laugh at. They together an hour, and by and by church-time, whither he led her into the coach and into the church, and so at church all the afternoon, several handsome ladies at church. But it was most extraordinary hot that ever I knew it. So home again and to walk in the gardens, where we left the young couple a second time. Anon to supper, and excellent discourse and dispute between my Lord Crew and the chaplin, who is a good scholler, but a nonconformist. After Mr. Carteret was carried to his chamber, we to prayers again and then to bed.

17th. Up all of us, and to billiards ; my Lady Wright, Mr. Carteret, myself, and every body. By and by the young couple left together. Anon to dinner ; and after dinner Mr. Carteret took my advice about giving to the servants, and I led him to give £10 among them, which he did, by leaving it to the chief man-servant, Mr. Medows, to do for him. Before we went, I took my Lady Jem. apart, and would know how she liked this gentleman, and whether she was under any difficulty concerning him. She blushed, and hid her face awhile ; but at last I forced her to tell me. She answered that she could readily obey what her father and mother had done ; which was all she could say, or I expect. So anon I took leave, and for London. But, Lord ! to see, among other things, how all these great people here are afeard of London (on account of the plague) that I was forced to say that I lived wholly at Woolwich. In our way Mr. Carteret did give me mighty thanks for my care and pains for him, and is mightily pleased, though the truth is, my Lady Jem. hath carried herself with mighty discretion and gravity, not being forward at all in any degree, but mighty serious in her answers to him, as by what he says and I observed, I collect. To London to my office, and so to Deptford, where mighty welcome, and brought the good newes of all being pleased to them. Mighty mirth at my giving them an account of all ; but the young man could not be got to say one word before me or my Lady Sandwich of his adventures, but by what he afterwards related to his father and mother and sisters, he gives an account that pleases them mightily. Here Sir G. Carteret would have me lie all night, which I did most nobly, better than ever I did in my life, Sir G. Carteret being mighty kind to me, leading me to my chamber ; and all their care now is to have the business ended, and they have reason, because the sicknesse puts all out of order, and they cannot safely stay where they are.

24th. By appointment to Deptford, to Sir G. Carteret's,

between six and seven o'clock, where I found him and my Lady almost ready, and by and by went over to the ferry, and took coach and six horses nobly for Dagenhams, himself and lady and their little daughter, Louisonne, and myself in the coach ; where, when we were come, we were bravely entertained and spent the day most pleasantly with the young ladies, and I so merry as never more. Only for want of sleep, and drinking of strong beer had a rheum in one of my eyes, which troubled me much. Here with great content all the day, as I think I ever passed a day in my life, because of the contentfulnesse of our errand, and the noblenesse of the company and our manner of going. But I find Mr. Carteret yet as backward almost in his caresses, as he was the first day. At night, about seven o'clock, took coach again, but, Lord ! to see in what a pleasant humour Sir G. Carteret hath been both coming and going ; so light, so fond, so merry, so boyish (so much content he takes in this business), it is one of the greatest wonders I ever saw in my mind. But once in serious discourse he did say that, if he knew his son to be a debauchee, as many and most are now-a-days about the Court, he would tell it, and my Lady Jem. should not have him.

28th. Up betimes, and down to Deptford. Set out with my Lady all alone with her with six horses to Dagenhams ; going by water to the Ferry. And a pleasant going, and good discourse ; and when there, very merry, and the young couple now well acquainted. But, Lord ! to see what fear all the people here do live would make one mad, they are afeard of us that come to them, insomuch that I am troubled at it, and wish myself away. But some cause they have ; for the chaplin, with whom but a week or two ago we were here mighty high disputing, is since fallen into a fever and dead, being gone hence to a friend's a good way off. A sober and healthful man. These considerations make us all hasten the marriage, and resolve it upon Monday next, which is three days before we intended it. Mighty merry all of us, and in the evening with full content took coach again and home by daylight with great pleasure.

31st. Up, and very betimes by six o'clock at Deptford, and there find Sir G. Carteret, and my Lady ready to go : I being in my new coloured silk suit, and coat trimmed with gold buttons and gold broad lace round my hands, very rich and fine. By water to the Ferry, where, when we come, no coach there; and tide of ebb so far spent as the horse-boat could not get off the other side the river to bring away the coach. So we were fain to stay there in the unlucky Isle of Doggs, in a chill place, the morning cool, and the wind fresh, above two if not three hours to our great discontent. Yet being upon a pleasant errand, and seeing that it could not be helped, we did bear it very patiently; and it was worth my observing, I thought, as ever any thing, to see how upon these two scores, Sir G. Carteret, the most passionate man in the world, and that was in the greatest haste to be gone, did bear with it, and very pleasant all the while, at least not troubled much so as to fret and storm at it. Anon the coach comes: we fearing the canonicall hour would be past before we got thither, did with a good deal of unwillingness send away the license and wedding ring. So that when we come, though we drove hard with six horses, yet we found them gone from home; and going towards the church, met them coming from church, which troubled us. But, however, that trouble was soon over; hearing it was well done: they both being in their old cloaths; my Lord Crew giving her, there being three coach fulls of them. The young lady mighty sad, which troubled me; but I think it was only her gravity in a little greater degree than usual. All saluted her, but I did not till my Lady Sandwich did ask me whether I had saluted her or no. So to dinner, and very merry we were; but yet in such a sober way as never almost any wedding was in so great families: but it was much better. After dinner company divided, some to cards, others to talk. My Lady Sandwich and I to settle accounts, and pay her some money. And mighty kind she is to me. At night to supper, and so to talk; and which, me-thought, was the most extraordinary thing, all of us to prayers as usual, and the young bride and bridegroom too: and so after prayers, soberly to bed; only I got into the bridegroom's chamber while he undressed himself, and there was very merry, till he was called to the bride's chamber, and into bed they went. I kissed the bride in bed, and so the curtaines drawne with the greatest gravity that could be, and so good night. But the modesty and gravity of this business was so decent, that it was to me indeed ten times more delightfull than if it had been twenty times more merry and joviall. Whereas I feared I must have sat up all night, we did here all get good beds, and I lay in the same I did before with Mr. Brisband, who is a good scholler and sober man ; and we lay in bed, getting him to give me an account of Rome, which is the most delightfull talke a man can have of any traveller : and so to sleep. My eyes much troubled already with the change of my drink. Thus I ended this month with the greatest joy that ever I did any in my life, because I have spent the greatest part of it with abundance of joy, and honour, and pleasant journeys, and brave entertainments, and without cost of money ; and at last live to see the business ended with great content on all sides. Myself having obliged both these families in this business very much ; as both my Lady, and Sir G. Carteret and his Lady do confess exceedingly, and the latter do also now call me cozen, which I am glad of. So God preserve us all friends long, and continue health among us.

Saffron

(Try it on the Crocodile)

FULLER : *History of the Worthies of England,* 1662

Plenty hereof in this County growing about *Walden* a fair Market Town, which *Saffron* may seem to have coloured with the name thereof. In it self it is a most admirable Cordiall, and, under God I owe my life, when sick of the small pox, to the efficacy thereof.

No precious drug is more adulterated with *Cartamus,* the *inward pilling of Willow,* and generally all yellow flowers, when it is bought in great parcells, which ought to quicken the care of Chapmen herein. In a word, the Soveraign Power of genuine *Saffron,* is plainly proved by the Antipathy of the *Crocodiles* thereunto. For the *Crocodiles tears* are never *true,* save when he forced where *Saffron* groweth, knowing himself to be all *Poison,* and it all *Antidote.*

Gabriel Harvey, 1545 ?–1630

Gabriel Harvey's Marginalia, ed. MOORE SMITH, 1913
T. NASHE : *Have with you to Saffron Walden,* 1596

England, since it was England, never bred more honorable minds, more adventurous hearts, more valourous hands, or more excellent wits than of late. . . .   The date of idle vanities is expired : away with these scribbling paltries : there is another Sparta in hand, that indeed requireth Spartan Temperance, Spartan Frugality, Spartan exercise, Spartan valiency, Spartan perseverance, Spartan invincibility. . . .

[Harvey was renowned in his day as a poet and scholar, and these are fine words which acquired a new pregnancy in 1940, but he was less happy in his description of his reception by Queen Elizabeth when she visited Audley End in 1578.]

> *The kingly hall I seek, and greet its Lord :*
> *He, when he saw me, gave me friendly words :*
> *" Stay, Harvey, thou shalt see Eliza soon :*
> *Eliza soon shall see thee and thy verses."*

Quick from her chamber came the Royal Virgin.
A star, I swear, more bright than stars themselves.
Kindly, and with ambrosial hand outstretched,
To me she grants a sweet kiss to impress,
A kiss more heavenly than heaven itself,
And almost more divine than deity.
   But when thay goodly star with splendour new
Had dazed my eyes . . . it is scarcely credible
With what profound emotion the Queen's words
Stirred my whole soul, with what divinity
Arrested all my being, as she said,
" Who is that man ? tell me, I pray, who is he ? "
And added, " Harvey, I will not deny
To thee my right hand." Oh, those queenly words
Are of more worth to me than great Apollo's,
And all the Muses nine and nine Minervas.
I dance with joy, and exultations new
My spirit thrill, such as no other day,
No happiest day had e'er before bestowed.

[This was his finest hour, when, according to his enemy Nashe, he was " Ruffling it out hufty-tufty in a suit of velvet." Later many sorrows fell upon him and there is pathos in Nashe's account of his old age.]

His complexion is of an adust swarth chollericke dye, like restie bacon, or a dride scate-fish : so leane and so meagre, that you wold thinke (like the Turks) he observ'd 4 Lents in a yere : his skin riddled and crumpled like a peice of burnt parchment. For his stature, he is such another pretie *Iacke a Lent* as boyes throw at in the streete, and lookes, in his blacke sute of velvet, like one of those ieat droppes which divers weare at their eares in stead of a jewell. A smudge peice of a handsome fellow it hath beene in his dayes, but now he olde and past his best, cares have so crazed him, and disgraces to the verie bones consumed him ; and if none of them were, his course of life is such as would make anie man looke ill on it, for he wil endure more hardnes than a Camell, who in the burning sands will live foure dayes without water & feedes on nothing but thistles and wormewood & such lyke ; no more doth he feed on anie thing, when he is at *Saffron-Walden*, but sheepes trotters, porknells, and buttered rootes ; and other-while in an Hexameter meditation, or hatching such another Paradoxe as that of *Nicholas Copernicus* was, who held that the Sun remains immoveable in the center of the World & that the Earth is moov'd about the Sunne, he would be so rapt that he would remaine three dayes and neither eate nor drinke, and within doores he will keepe seaven yeare together, and come not abroad so much as to Church.

SAINT OSYTH

FULLER : *History of the Worthies of England,* 1662

Saint OSITH. She was daughter to the King of the *East Angles*, and wife to *Suthred* last King of *East-Saxons*, by whose consent forsaking the world, she was *veiled*, and at last became Abbess of a Monastery of her own founding at *Chich* in this County ; until the *Danes* infesting these sea-coasts, cut off her head in hatred of Religion.

Yet this her head, after it was cut off was carried by Saint *Osith* (*oh wonder ! oh lie !*) *three furlongs*, and then she fell down and died. The same *mutatis mutandis* is told of Saint *Dionys* in *France*, Saint *Winefride* in *Wales* and others, such being the barrenness of Monkish invention, that unable to furnish their severall Saints with a variety of fictions, their tired fancie is fain to make the same miracle serve many Saints. She was martyred about the year of our Lord 870.

AUBREY : *Anecdotes and Traditions,* Camden Society, 1839

In those dayes (tpe Mariae Reginae) when they went to bed they did rake up the fire and make a + in the ashes, and pray to God and St. *Sythe* to deliver them from fire and from water, and from all misadventure.

Mice Devour the Grasse in Danesey

J. STOW : *Annales*, 1615

About Hallontide 1580, in the marishes of Danesey Hundred, in a place called Southminster in the countie of Essex, a strange thing hapned : there sodainlie appeared an infinite multitude of mice, which overwhelming the whole earth in the saide marishes, did sheare and gnaw the grasse by the rootes, spoyling and tainting the same with their venimous teeth, in such sort, that the cattell which grazed thereon were smitten with a murreine and died thereof, which vermine by policie of man could not be destroyed, till at the last it came to passe that there flocked together all about the same marishes, such a number of owles, as all the shire was able to yeeld : whereby the marsh-holders were shortly delivered from the vexation of the said mice.

Disaffection in 1592

Essex County Session Rolls, Hist. MSS. Com., 10th Report

The Examination, before Sir Edward Huddleston knt, of William Clarke of Holborne, London, touching contumelious words alleged to have been spoken to him by a sailor, on the highway between Chelmsforde and Witham, about Springfield, which sailor, on being asked whether he had come over with the Lord Thomas Howard answered for himself and two other sailors accompanying him, that " they cam over with an honester man then Lorde Thomas Howarde " adding " Hange him villeine, for he hath cast awaie a number of men better then himsealf."

[The sailor was apparently Francis Foorde, of Ipswich. It will be remembered that Lord Thomas Howard in 1591 sailed away from Flores with five ships of war, leaving Sir Richard Grenville in the *Revenge* to face the Spanish fleet alone.]

The Whitsuntide Singers

I. HOLST : *Gustav Holst*, 1938

In 1914 Gustav Holst left London and came to live at Thaxted, in a three-hundred-year-old cottage on the top of a hill. The valley was planted with young willow trees, and a high wind would turn them to silver. And in the distance the spire of Thaxted Church stood up against the sky.

Thaxted itself was beautiful, and the church was the crowning glory of the place. It was like a cathedral. And inside, instead of being dark and cluttered up, it was spacious and incredibly light.

Standing in those empty aisles, and seeing the shafts of sunlight slanting through the pillars, Holst dreamed of a festival of music that might happen there one day. He would bring down his pupils, past and present, from Morley College and St. Paul's Girls' School, and they would do " Sleepers Wake " and " Soul, Array Thyself," and Palestrina and Vittoria and Purcell.

The dream was realised during the Whitsun week-end of 1916, and when it was over he described it in a letter to his friend, W. G. Whittaker :

" I would have written before, but I was so tied up with our musical festival (or rather feast) at Thaxted last week.

" It *was* a feast—an orgy. Four whole days of perpetual singing and playing, either properly arranged in the church or impromtu in various houses or still more impromptu in ploughed fields during thunderstorms, or in the train going home.

" In the intervals between the services people drifted into the church and sang motets or played violin or 'cello. And others caught bad colds through going long walks in the pouring rain singing madrigals and folk songs and rounds the whole time."

He also wrote :

" I realise now why the bible insists on heaven being a place

(I should call it a condition) where people sing and *go on singing*.

"We kept it up at Thaxted about fourteen hours a day. The reason we didn't do more is that we were not capable mentally or physically of realising heaven any further.

"Still, as far as it went it was heaven. Just as the average amateur's way of using music as a sedative or a stimulant is purgatory, and the professional's way of using music as a topic of conversation or as a means of getting money is hell.

"Music, being identical with heaven, isn't a thing of momentary thrills, or even hourly ones. It is a condition of eternity."

Life at Hill Hall in November 1914

JOSEPH HONE : *Life of Henry Tonks,* 1939

Tonks went to Hill Hall in Essex in order to put his medical knowledge at the service of Mr. and Mrs. Charles Hunter, who had opened a hospital for wounded officers and were extending their hospitality to French and Belgian refugees. . . . Once at luncheon to the great delight of Mrs. Hunter's grand-children Tonks gave a realistic representation of a Belgian soldier's wounded toe, with the help of a banana. . . . Rodin and Madame Rodin were among the refugees but Tonks did not disguise his disappointment with Rodin, " Why I have never heard him say anything except ' Dieu que les arbres sont beaux.' "

Bewilderment in August 1914

ARNOLD BENNETT : *Journals*, vol. 2, 1932

Thorpe-le-Soken, Thursday, August 6th

On arriving at Brightlingsea on Monday afternoon, I was told that petrol could not be got in the district ; that it was fetching up to 10s. a tin at Clacton ; and that Baggaley, the regular hirer of motor cars at Brightlingsea, had gone forth in an attempt to get petrol.

At Clacton yesterday the price was 2s. 3d. or 2s. 4d. a gallon. I have 60 gallons in stock.

A great crowd of holiday makers at Clacton in the showers yesterday. No difficulty about getting change for a £10 note in gold and silver. At the fish shop, slight increases of price in poultry and eggs. The man said he expected to get no more fish after that day.

Yesterday we heard noises of explosions destroying inconvenient houses at Harwich. The sensations of the Harwich people must be poignant.

An officer came yesterday to complain of a fox terrier (? ours) which flew at dispatch riders on motor bicycles. He said it would be shot if it was found loose. These dispatch-riders are the most picturesque feature of the war here. They rush through the village at speeds estimated up to 50 miles an hour, I am willing to concede 40.

Edith Johnston recounts how her father is laying in ammunition against the time when the people will raid the countryside demanding provisions ; he, being a farmer, is to be called on early in the proceedings, and is determined to give out his stores evenly and not to the strongest. Each morning he summons all his men and explains to them the course of the war, so that they shall not be misled by rumours. Edith thinks that a war is necessary and advisable, as the population is too thick.

[From the Tollesbury Parish Registers.]

August 30th, 1718. Elizabeth, daughter of Robert and Eliza Wood, being the first Childe whom was baptized in the New Font which was bought out of five pounds paid by John Norman, who some few months before came drunk into the church and cursed and talked loud in the time of Divine Service, to prevent his being prosecuted for which he paid by agreement the above said five pounds. Note that the wise rhymes on the font were put there by the sole order of Robert Joyce then Churchwarden.

[The " wise rhymes " are :

> Good people all I pray take care
> That in ye church you do not swear,
> As this man did.]

The Tadpole of a Motorist

Dr. Salter of Tolleshunt D'Arcy, His Diary and Reminiscences, 1849–1932,
ed. J. O. THOMPSON, 1933

1897

March 25. A motor-car came through the village under the management of Mr. Wellington and called at my house. I was given a ride to Salcott turning and back. We went at the rate of 12 or 14 miles an hour ! I was exceedingly attracted by the thing. It cost £300 to build.

March 27. Went 13 miles by the car in five minutes under the hour, stopping twice for ten minutes to show the machine. All the world came out to stare at us as we went along. We went down some of the hills at the rate of 20 miles an hour ! the motion was delightful and quite sleigh-like.

1901

Jan. 11. Got nearly smashed by a motor-car, which class of goods " Taffy " [his horse] can't abide.

Oct. 19. Went riding round in George Fisher's motor-car. The motor riding is most exhilarating, and saves much time.

Nov. 18. Up at 4 a.m., cup of coffee, and at 5 George Fisher appeared punctually at the door with his motor-car to give me a run to Hertford to shoot at Brickendonbury. We reached Bradwell in an hour, and then had to pull up for forty minutes to " put something right "—the morning cold, frosty, and dark, the roads good. We then went on again, passed through Braintree and Rayne without adventure, but still the thing did not appear to be " spinning." Presently we had another breakdown. Sometimes it was the " carburetter," sometimes the electric explosion—then this, then that, until my driver became quite obfuscated. I believe it was the bad " petrol " from beginning to end. Well, we reached Dunmow and Bishop's Stortford without an actual breakdown, though one of the wheels very nearly came off, and it would have been awkward if it had done so as we sped down those hills ! We then came to Hadham, a pretty village, and then to Widford, where our miseries culminated in a complete stop. Poor George was at his wit's end, and did not know what to do, so enlisting the sympathies of a passing travelling draper named Johnson, living in the neighbourhood of Hatfield Heath, and finding there was a motor-shop at Ware, about five miles distant on our road, I got him to drive me with his little go-cart and Russian pony which I could stop with the Russian " note," but he could not make him go with all his English persuasion, to Ware, where I found that George had got there first by another road. I went on by the same conveyance, slow and not very sure, to Brickendonbury, where I arrived at 1.30, just in time to join the shooters and scrap up a bit of luncheon, the first bite I had had since leaving home— and then shot for the rest of the afternoon.

I killed 46 pheasants, went to the house, had some tea, and caught the 5.40 train from Hertford. Having wired and received a wire from George Fisher, who met me at Ware for a moment's chat as the train stopped, we arranged that he should stay the night at Ware and return tomorrow. I got some food in the grillroom at Liverpool Street Station, and home by the mail, hiring from Kelvedon. All hands were relieved and astonished to see me return in this way, though they had had their forebodings all day !

1902
Jan. 1. Sent back from Witham at night on a motor. Rather a pleasant experience, going fast through the night air.

April 28. Had a delightful round in G. Fisher's motor-car— 60 miles, and not a hitch.

May 12. G. Fisher promised me a trip round in his motor, but he could not get the thing to " go." I therefore drove down and saw some patients at Tollesbury first. I joined him then about 12.30. We now went at a good speed and smoothly. Coming out of Birch Rectory grounds, and going much too fast in turning the corner, we capsized and it was a mercy we weren't both killed on the spot. He was under the machine, with debris scattered all over the road ; I was shied against the bank, and got off with some bruises. After a bit we got the thing going again and went on our rounds, but not as far as I had intended.

May 13.   Barring being a bit stiff, and having a large map of the world on my thigh and buttock, I was not much the worse for yesterday's spill.

July 15.   Beginning to see more and more how a motor-car would simplify my work.

July 24.   A long chat with William Moss on motor-cars, and got somewhat nearer to the proprietorship of one.

July 25.   Introduced by J. W. Moss to a young fellow at Feering who undertook to look for a motor-car for me.   They explained the mechanism of a Benz which was in the yard, and I got on very well with my first lesson.

July 28.   In response to a telegram went to London to look at a motor—a Benz ideal, 4½ horse power.   After some alterations and putting to rights of the motor, I paid for the car, and with a driver to take us out of the traffic of London, started for home.   We then sailed away—the car went beautifully.   We unshipped our pilot at Romford, and came on by ourselves.   It appears to be a first-class machine—cost me £239 5s.

July 29.   Had to forfeit, on account of work in the car, Provincial Grand Lodge at Chelmsford.   I was also unable to attend the Bench for the same reason, so that it was a day of hard work under *motor influence*.

July 30.   Horse exercise today instead of motor work.

July 31.   Forty-odd miles in 3½ hours.   I " took the ribbons " about a mile from D'Arcy, and drove home at a slow pace.

Aug. 7.   My motor man not turning up in time, I had to start with the Russian horse to get through my work, leaving him to follow if he came.   He did come, and he followed but did not catch me all day ; in fact I got home an hour before him, although he had been out with the car all day !

Sept. 2.   Over 70 miles in the car without a mishap—lovely travelling.

Sept. 23.   The motor behaved splendidly ; lit my acetylene lamp for the first time—first rate.

1903

April 21.   At the Witham Bench had a motor case for the first time ; and expressed my views rather openly—also about the practice of leaving horses unattended.

Master Gregory Cromwell Writes to His Father, Thomas Cromwell, later Chief Secretary to the King's Majesty and Earl of Essex

ELLIS : *Original Letters*, vol. 1, Series 3, 1835

Right worschypfull father, I comend me un to you, desiring you of your daily blessing, certifying you that I am in good health, with my cousins Bersfourd and Wellyfyd, thanks be to God omnipotent, and apply our books diligently, as shall appear I trust to your worship and our profits. Father, I beseech you when ye meet with the right honourable lord of Oxford, to give thanks to his Lordship, for when he came to a town called Yeldham, to the parsons there of to hunt the fox, he sent for me and my cousins, and made us good cheer ; and let us see such game and pleasure as I never saw in my life ; more over father, I beseech you to give thanks to the fore said parson of Yeldham, which since I came in to the country hath divers times sent for me and for my cousins and made us high cheer, and showed us great pleasure. For all other things concerning my raiment, I beseech you give credence to my singular good friend Master Doctor Lee. Thus Jesu have you in his keeping. From Topsfyld the xvii day of October. By your lowly son

GREGORY CRUMWELL

To hys ryght worschypfull father
  Master Crumwell be thys yevne.

[This is believed to be one of the earliest references to fox-hunting in England. Gregory was probably about twelve years old when he wrote this polite and charming letter. He evidently went to Mr. Becansawe, rector of Toppesfield, for his education.

The last wild boar in Essex is reputed to have been killed near Earls Colne in the reign of Queen Elizabeth by a later Earl of Essex.

R. S. R. FITTER : *London's Natural History*, 1945]

" Good Old Days " on the Marshes

S. BARING GOULD : *Mehalah*, 1880

At the time of the Napoleonic wars, the mouth of the Black-water was a great centre of the smuggling trade. It was easy for those who knew the creeks to elude the revenue boats, and every farm and tavern was ready to give cellarage to run goods and harbour to smugglers. Deeds of violence were not rare and many a revenue officer who attempted to arrest and detain contraband goods fell victim to his zeal. On Sunken Island off Mersea, the story went, that a whole boat's crew were found with their throats cut ; they were transported thence to the churchyard, there buried, and their boat turned keel upwards over them.

The villages of Virley and Salcot were the chief landing-places for smuggled goods, and there horses and donkeys were kept in large numbers for the conveyance of the spirits, wine, tobacco and silk to Tiptree Heath, which was the emporium of the trade.

Virley Church possessed but one bell, which was tolled alike for weddings and funerals ; there was a difference in the pace at which it went for these distinct solemnities, but that was all. The bell produced neither a cheerful nor a lugubrious effect on either occasion, as it was cracked. The dedication of Virley Church is unknown—no doubt because it never had a patron ; or if it had, the patron disowned it. No saint in the calendar could be associated with such a church and keep his character.

The altar was a deal table, much wormeaten, with a box beneath it. The altar possessed no cover save the red cotton handkerchief of the curate cast occasionally across it.

The Communion rails had rotted at the bottom ; and when there was a Communion the clerk had to caution the kneelers not to lean against the balustrade, lest they should be precipitated upon the sanctuary floor.

No such controversy as that which has of late years agitated the Church of England relative to the position of the celebrant could have affected Virley, for the floor in the midst, before the altar, had been eaten through by rats, emerging from an old grave, and exposed below gnawed and mouldy bones a foot beneath the boards.

Though the church sometimes contained a congregation, it never held one of worshippers. The youths who attended divine worship on Sundays occupied the hour of worship by wafting kisses to the girls, making faces at the children, and scratching ships on the paint of the pews. Indeed, the religious services might have been discontinued, without discomposure to any, had not traditional usage consecrated them to the meeting of young couples. The " dearly beloveds " met in the Lord's house every Lord's day to acknowledge their " erring and straying like lost sheep " and make appointments for erring and straying again.

Great Waltham Parks in the Fifteenth Century

From the Court Rolls of the Manor of Waltham Bury

E. R. CLARK : " Great Waltham Five Centuries Ago," *E.R.*, vol. xiii

There were three parks, each enclosed with an unbroken cincture of paling, the Old Park, Apechild [now Absol] Park, and Lytel-hey [now Littley] Park. Each park was in charge of two officers, the *parcarius* and the *paliciarius*. The parcarius had charge of the timber and looked out for trespassers after fish or game ; the paliciarius found his occupation in keeping the palings in good order ; and they had joint charge of the cattle and pigs grazing in the park, by means of nick-stick or talley. In English both the officers seen to have been called " parker."

The " parker of Apechild " held freely 9 acres of land ; he had for further perquisite whatever portions of the new felled timber were unsuitable for pales and whatever portions of the old pales were unsuitable for mending the fence : also the right to have five grazing animals in the park throughout the whole year, and five pigs at pasture there except during the month when pigs are excluded from the park. In return he was to keep up the paling.

The homage kept a sharp look out on the parker's work and a constantly recurring precept is that the paling of Apechild park is to be repaired before next court day under penalty of 20s. or 40s. In March 1411, William Shergot, called to book for carrying off part of the pales at Mychelles-pond, confessed to taking a pale blown down by the wind, and was fined 6d.

The Court Baron kept a jealous eye not only on trees felled, and their toppings, but also of boughs blown down by the wind, and of the undergrowth. In January 1395, the parker of Apechild, Thomas Couland, reported delivering to the reeve of the Manor, two oaks and one branch for the repairs of the lord's mills, and in July of the same year, to felling of twelve oaks for repairs at the " new College " at Plessitz. In May 1397 four oaks were felled " for the bay next the kitchen "

[? at Pleshey Castle] and one oak for making a bridge at Waltham Manor. In October 1398 the homage presented the sale by William Harecoarte, now parker, of one ash, one maple, one old oak, and firewood, all blown down by the wind, to the end that the Steward might enquire whether Harecoarte had accounted for the proceeds. In January 1399, the Court ordered the sale of " one lop of oak " blown down, for 40d. ; and sold at the rate of 1d. per perch the hedge growth of the old hedge in Absol Park.

Especially interesting is the felling (January 1404) of four ashes in Absol park by order of the Treasurer of the Lady of the Manor's household, to be made into tallies by which to reckon the expenses of the household.

[The destruction of the old House of Commons in 1834 was caused by the burning of old medieval tallies.]

A Clerical Duet

E. DURRANT : " Reminiscences of Old Chelmsford," *E.R.*, vol. ix

Mention of the old Chelmsford Gaol near Moulsham Bridge reminds me that a reverend prisoner the vicar of Great Waltham, was confined there in 1823, for a very unusual offence. That gentleman, the Rev. G. S. Clarke by name, was a learned if eccentric scholar, who insisted upon giving his own translations of various portions of the Bible when reading the lessons in his church. Being requested by the bishop to conform to the authorised version, he refused. He was then inhibited, and a substitute despatched to conduct his services. Mr. Clarke, however, persisted, and continued to read and perform his office at one end of the church, while the bishop's nominee was in the act of doing so at the other. For this contumacious conduct the vicar was finally suspended, and removed to a room over the gateway of the prison, which he called Caukwell Hall from the name of the Governor.

Furniture for the Earl of Essex's Cell in the Tower of London, 11 February, 1601

Shirley MSS., R. Com. on Hist. MSS., 5th Report

[Robert Devereux, 2nd Earl of Essex. He had bought Wanstead from Lord Rich in 1577.]

Essex being now a prisoner in the Tower is unfurnished of these things here-under written.

Deliver to the bearer Geo. Partridge servant to Mr. Lieutenant : A table for himself and another for the outward chamber, a carpet for his table, a foot carpet for the floor, two cushions, a pair of silver candlesticks, a chamber pot, a fire shovel and tongs, a pair of bellows, a pan to burn rosewater, bedding for Mr. Warbert and his man ; a silver salt and spoon, two silver pots for wine.

These received by Partridge, and two hangings more.

[Essex, young and handsome and favourite of Queen Elizabeth, was beheaded in the Tower a fortnight later. Had there been some premonition of his fate when, returning victorious from the sacking of Cadiz, at the height of his power and glory, he had written the following simple and pathetic lines?]

A Passion of My Lo. of Essex

Fullers Worthies Library, ed. GROSART, 1872

Happy were he could finish forth his fate
  In some unhaunted desert, most obscure
From all society, from love and hate
  Of worldly folks ; there might he sleep secure.
There walke again, and give God ever praise,
  Content with hips and haws, and brambleberry,
In contemplation passing still his days,
  And change of holy thoughts to make him merry ;
That when he dies his tomb might be a bush
  Where harmless Robin dwells with gentle thrush.

Home Defence in 1778

ASPINAL–OGLANDER : *Admiral's Widow*, 1943

[The Duke of Beaufort's Monmouth Fusiliers were training at Warley Camp with other bodies of Militia and Volunteers. His Grace was in command of the regiment, and letters from his mother-in-law, Mrs. Boscawen, describe some of the scenes there. She was a great-niece of John Evelyn and had much of his charm and learning.]

18th August, 1778.

The Duchess of Beaufort is already set out from Badminton, and though she makes a coasting voyage, going with the Duke to Salisbury, Winchester, Lymington and finally to Brighton, yet I think it will end in London early in the next week, from whence the Duke will join his new levies and march them into camp at Warley, and the Duchess with two elder girls, will come and stay 3 days with me, during which time a small mansion near Warley Camp will be prepared for her reception. It is called Howe Hatch, she tells me, and I found it on the map.

Howe Hatch.

13th October, 1778.

You judged very truly my dear Fanny, that it would be almost impossible to find the writing hour at this place, for we are out all the morning, and, in the evening have company, or, if not, a *tête-à-tête* with my dear hostess [her daughter the Duchess].

Yesterday we had a rehearsal of the battle (*la grande journée*) that is to be performed before the King and Queen next Tuesday. I saw it, and at first it was charming, viz. all the regiments marching by the General (near whom we were placed) and saluting him ; music playing etc. But when the battle began *avec un feu terrible and continuel*, with the cannons brazen mouths, it was so tremendous that we wish'd ourselves at home again. However we stayed till the hurly burly was done and the feigned battle stoutly won. Then we took but half the *feu de joie* for the victory, the other half being performed much too near us.

I have been at Lord Petre's twice, where I saw the magnificence with which his Lordship—quite *en Prince*—has prepared for his royal guests.

[A year later Mrs. Boscawen was again with her daughter, but this time at Hunton House.]

9th Sept., 1779.

My noble host is so entirely taken up with his military business, as he commands all the Grenadiers of the camp as well as his own Regiment, that we see him only at dinner and supper, so that my dear hostess and I being alone the rest of the day, we do not part longer than dressing or the very necessary writing requires, but read and work together, and in the afternoon constantly take an airing up to the camp, which is about a mile off, and there stay till the evening gun announces the piquet guard, when the music plays. Some of the bands are very fine.

There is an immense public room, made of tarpaulin and built in a week. There are two balls in a week, and other nights conversation and music and (I suppose) cards.

A Charter of Edward the Confessor, 1046

BENHAM : " Manorial Rolls of Fingringhoe, West Mersea and
Pete Hall," *E.R.*, vol. li

In the name of the highest thunderer, namely the Almighty
God who hath formed all things out of nothing, and who established the first-born man, Adam, to be as it were a fellow-
citizen of the heavenly Jerusalem, and who, with enormous compassion and fore-ordinance brought him forth to the summit of
Angelic bliss, redeemed by His very own blood, as it is now
needful to all Christian men, as long as they may continue in
mortal life, to exchange heavenly things for the things that shall
perish, eternal things for things which are transient.

I, King Edward, am strengthened in this counsel, because the
same (Word of) Truth says, "Give and it shall be given unto
you," and also the Scripture admonishes "The ransom of a man's
soul are his riches," and Solomon " Son, giving of alms delivers
the soul from death and suffers it not to depart into darkness."

Whereupon, helped by the support of these precepts and of
others, I, Edward, above designated as head of the English and
the Northumbrians, give to the Lord King of all Kings, and to
Saint Peter and also to the blessed abbot Audoen (or Ouen, in
Normandy) and to those serving him, who has hitherto been
the special patron of my ancestors, a certain part of the island
which is called *Merseye*, with meadows and woods with rights
of fishery, as I had this entire and in possession in the course of
two days after, by the grace of God, I attained to the beginning
of my reign.

And truly if any person among men shall attempt to invali-
date this my gift, let him know that before Christ and the
Angels, and the beforewritten Saints, he shall be called to
terrible account and utterly damned, unless he shall here fully
make restitution.

This aforesaid gift is made in the year of the Lord's Incarna-
tion one thousand and forty-six.

Sealed by the King and witnessed and confirmed by 19 of
his Archbishops, Bishops, Abbots, Officers and Magnates.

John Skelton, to Mistress Margery Wentworth, of Codham Hall

Garlande of Laurell, 1523

With margerain gentle,
  The flower of goodlihood,
Embroidered the mantle
  Is of your maidenhood.

Plainly, I cannot glose [flatter]
  Ye be, as I divine,
The pretty primerose,
  The goodly columbine.

Benign, courteous, and meek,
  With wordes well devised,
In you, who list to seek,
  Be virtues well comprised.

With margerain gentle,
  The flower of goodlihood,
Embroidered the mantle
  Is of your maidenhood.

A Miracle, 5 March, 1490

The Miracles of King Henry VI. Twenty-three Miracles taken from the Manuscript in the British Museum, translated by RONALD KNOX

With amazement we have heard of what was done in these last days at a place called *Whyt Rodyng*, within the borders of Essex, through the patronage of the most glorious and most holy King Henry. There was a man there of honorable birth and rank, called Robert Pokeapart : and it was a young servant of his, who experienced the wonderful power which the aforesaid man of God had in the name of Christ.

This young man had come home after a long interval from the famous town of London, with two companions only—one who was driving, and another young man called Dominic Pokeapart. All three together were following a loaded waggon, which contained two casks of salt fish and a considerable amount of rocksalt. So, while they occupied themselves in their customary stories and trifles walking beside the waggon, with all too little care for themselves and their own fortunes, a sudden accident befell them. Quite unexpected the waggon upset, and in falling crushed beneath it the young man whom we have mentioned. So violently did it hurl him to the ground as to prevent the breath of life from remaining longer in him—and no wonder ; the whole impact of the entire weight so leaned upon him that, had it been ten times less, it might have broken a man's back by the force of it. What need to say more ? There stood the two companions, terribly shocked by the untoward happening, and indescribably confused between feeling of alarm and grief, all the brightness gone from their faces, scarce able to control themselves. Poor fellows, what could they do ? They were quite alone, although on a public thoroughfare, with no knowledge of any remedy that could be applied. The weight, of course, was too much for their strength ; yet they tried, by holding their breath and eking out force with art—and that a force which panic had lent them beyond the use of nature—to drag out their companion's body from under the waggon. When they had succeeded in this, just at the moment when they might have expected some relief, all hopes of relief proved to have disappeared ; there was no trace of life remaining in him. They put their heads together, feeling they must act cautiously, or some ill-disposed person might come along and suspect them of murder, or at least reprove them for having let the accident happen through their own carelessness ; so they hurridly drew him away from the road and hid him under some thick bushes. This was about three in the afternoon. But I must not forget to mention one thing. I suppose that one of them must have been granted a special inspiration : for, before they left, he implored the pity of Almighty God with tearful face and asking the aid of Mary, the great and incomparable Mother of God, and the said glorious King Henry, he bent a penny double [a common habit in making a vow] which he promised faithfully to carry to his tomb. He, no doubt was less troubled over his dead friend than over his own safety, fearing though unnecessarily, the arm of the Law. What then ? They collected their wares and put them back on the waggon, and went off with all haste, their natural sorrow forgotten in their innocent fears. And so coming home, and finding their guardian, Robert, whom we have mentioned already, they took him aside without a moments delay and told him the cause of their unhappiness : without saying a word to any other, or even letting themselves be seen by any other, they went and hid themselves safely until the matter should have found its issue.

Robert Pokeapart, when he had heard the story, shewed the impression it had made on him by action. . . . He waited till morning, for their was no suitable opportunity till then, nor did there seem any need of haste, since there was no hope that Wall could come to life : then he took with him several of his immediate neighbours and found the corpse, and had it carried back to the town making no little lament over it ; there he had it publicly exposed to view, lest any breath of ill suspicion might bring any man to condemnation. The townspeople, when the dead man had been thus openly exhibited to them by the space of four hours, could entertain no hope for him : yet urged thereto by the very excess of their bitter grief conceived no less in affection for the young man than in horror of the occurrence, they all turned their eyes upward and gazed towards heaven ; all stretched out their hands on high, and beseiged the hearing of the Heavenly King with loud and heartfelt cries. And they added especially the humble mention of King Henry's memory, praying he would give them relief.

It was timely done ; a miracle followed thereupon worthy of all admiration. There was no question of the lad raving through any trance or any wandering of his wits ; he had been overtaken by a shocking and sudden fate, and had remained now, his whole body stiff, for almost twenty hours : and now it might be seen how little power has any calamity, even death itself, against the prayers of the faithful and the merits of the Saints, he broke through the bonds of death and appeared living. At that instant he became safe and sound, and was not backward in extolling continually the praises of King Henry, speaking of his merits more often and with more devotion than of any thing besides. And truly he had reason ; for from that time he had no need of any bodily medicine, save only to ensure that the health and strength of body restored to him by so notable a miracle should be protected with some care. Lest this act of the Most High should be concealed, or in any wise should pass into oblivion, both the master, Robert, and the lad's own father, and moreover that Dominic whom we have already mentioned, hastened to go with himself, before ten days had passed, to the sacred tomb of the glorious King Henry, and made the Church of Christ full of rejoicing, not so much over their alms as over the renown of the miracle.

The Green Children

T. KEIGHTLEY : *The Fairy Mythology*, 1850

" Another wonderful thing," says Ralph of Coggeshall, " happened in Suffolk, at St Mary's of the Wolf-pits. A boy and his sister were found by the inhabitants of that place near the mouth of a pit which is there, who had the form of all their limbs like to those of other men, but they differed in the colour of their skin from all the people of our habitable world ; for the whole surface of their skin was tinged of a green colour. No one could understand their speech. When they were brought as curiosities to the house of a certain knight, Sir Richard de Calne, at Wikes, they wept bitterly. Bread and other victuals were set before them, but they would touch none of them, though they were tormented by great hunger, as the girl afterwards acknowledged. At length, when some beans just cut, with their stalks, were brought into the house, they made signs, with great avidity, that they should be given to them. When they were brought, they opened the stalks instead of the pods, thinking the beans were in the hollow of them ; but not finding them there, they began to weep anew. When those who were present saw this, they opened the pods, and showed them the naked beans. They fed on these with great delight, and for a long time tasted no other food. The boy, however, was always languid and depressed, and he died within a short time. The girl enjoyed continual good health ; and becoming accustomed to various kinds of food, lost completely that green colour, and gradually recovered the sanguine habit of her entire body. She was afterwards regenerated by the laver of holy baptism, and lived for many years in the service of that knight (as I have frequently heard from him and his family), and was rather loose and wanton in her conduct. Being frequently asked about the people of her country, she asserted that the inhabitants, and all they had in that country, were of a green colour ; and that they saw no sun, but enjoyed a degree of light like what is after sunset. Being asked how she came into this country with the aforesaid boy, she replied, that as they were following their flocks, they came to a certain cavern, on entering which they heard a delightful sound of bells ; ravished by whose sweetness, they went for a long time wandering on through the cavern, until they came to its mouth. When they came out of it, they were struck senseless by the excessive light of the sun, and the unusual temperature of the air ; and thus they lay for a long time. Being terrified by the noise of those who came on them, they wished to fly, but they could not find the entrance of the cavern before they were caught.

[The story is also told by William of Newbridge, who places it in the reign of King Stephen. He says they said their country was called St. Martin's Land, as that saint was chiefly worshipped there ; that the people were Christians, and had churches ; that the sun did not rise there, but that there was a bright country which could be seen from theirs, being divided from it by a very broad river.]

A Country Estate in Victorian Times

Life of John Oxley Parker, 1812–1887, of Woodham Mortimer Place, J.P., D.L., and High Sheriff of Essex

And now let me give some description of life at Woodham Mortimer Place. The day began at 6 a.m., when John Barker, the Head Stockman, walked round the house ringing a large Hand Bell to awaken everybody. The coachman, Barthrop, was in his place in the Stables and had the cob, Topsy, ready for father to ride round farms. Aylett, the head wheelwright, rang a large bell, hung above his workshop, every morning at 6 a.m. for labourers. In the Carpenters' Shop there was James Falconer, with an assistant, and George Jenkins and his son George, who walked over every day from the Slough Wood, three miles. Brown was the blacksmith, and he had two assistants, for all the waggons and Tumbrels carts were made on the place by Aylett, and roads had in those days to be kept in order and gravel hauled from the gravel pits. At one time we had three Gamekeepers to look after about 4,000 acres of shooting, reaching from Jenkins', below Hazeleigh Hall, the Rectory Wood, Slough, Thrift Wood, the Wilderness, and all right away to Limeman Brook.

The gardeners were old Smee (Head Gardener), who always wore a top hat and a black frock coat, and his nephew Edward, and Mayhew, who was responsible to keep lawns cut with scythes and paths well swept. Old Smee was a tall man, with a Duke of Wellington nose. He lived in the Lodge on the way to the Rectory, and his wife managed our laundry.

The hackney stables were opposite the back door in the yard, and there 16 horses and ponies were kept. Wm. Baltrop, the head coachman, kept a shop in the village, in the cherry orchard, and his wife was cook at the Grange until she married Baltrop. Under him was John Jordan, the groom, who lived in the house, in a room beyond the Laundry, and shared by the Butler, William Wright, who had Billy Barr, a boy, or footman, under him ; Joe Read, Moses Ayres, strappers. William Wright taught us to ride and play cricket.

The horses kept were two pairs of carriage horses—one pair for use of the barouche, and the other, a lighter pair, bred by Father, were used seperately for light carts, or as a pair for the charabanc, or railway carriage as it was called.

In the main Stable were six horses ; in the farmyard at the end of the yard were the 3-stall stables, where Father's hunters at Oxford stood, and opposite this 3-stall stable was 2-stall loose boxes ; beyond this was a Cowshed for a herd of 15.

There was a similar herd of 15 cows at the Oak Farm, and at each farm a number of bullocks were fattened for Christmas, and it was a regular custom to inspect these fattening bullocks on Sundays before lunch. In the yard beyond the barn was Lucking's bricklayer's shop, and away in the 10 acres a shed for our Ponies or Hunters, turned out for the summer, and a small yard which two hunting horses run in and out of.

I can remember a few of the old labourers wearing smocks and under them breeches and short leather gaiters. At 8 a.m. they all came to have beer, allowed and put into small kegs, and then beer was always on tap during the day for any who liked to come for it.

The Birth of Broadcasting. "Two Emma Tock, Writtle Calling!"

P. P. ECKERSLEY : *The Power behind the Microphone*, 1941

When the war ended at last I found myself, in common with many other ex-officers, undecided what to do. Opportunity seemed infinite, it was the " dawn of a new era," our land was being made " fit for heroes to live in." It was clear to me, however, that I was not a hero and, pending the dawn, I had better set about getting a job. C. E. Prince, now my immediate boss at the R.A.F. Wireless Experimental Establishment wanted me to join with him in an Aircraft Section of the Marconi Company, which he and H. B. T. Childs hoped to be allowed to form. I joined the Marconi Company.

A few months later it was decided to move the technical section of the Aircraft Department from London to somewhere near Chelmsford. Prince decided he disliked a clay soil, so I was put in charge of the technical development. Our laboratory in Essex consisted of an army hut in a field, near the village of Writtle. . . .

We received a letter from head office saying that the amateurs, in the form of the Radio Society of Great Britain, wanted the Marconi Company to design, install and maintain a station on their behalf and that we had better do the job at Writtle. Naturally we were not to interrupt our normal work and, in any case, because the amateurs also had " normal work " it was no good transmitting before they got back to their homes. It was decided therefore to broadcast from eight to eight-thirty in the evening once a week. We received a little extra pay to do a little extra work and set about, rather lightheartedly, putting together some valves, condensers, and chokes " on a board " to produce the required low power transmitter. This was to be the first broadcasting station in Great Britain to do regular and advertised transmissions. But we only thought of it as another job of work for which we would be blamed if it went wrong and hardly noticed if it went right. But our critics, the wireless amateurs, were numerous and informed. They were liable to be rude if we were not efficient.

Our programmes were, at first, very formal. They were made up entirely of gramophone records. A mechanical gramophone played the music into the air and one of the staff held an ordinary microphone, such as one talks into when telephoning, in front of the trumpet.

(Later) began the Writtle programmes, remarkable for their gaiety and irresponsibility.

We signed off with a theme song. I sang it in a high tenor voice to the tune of Tosti's " Goodbye " with an accompaniment vamped on a piano.

> *Dearest, the concert's ended, sad wails the heterodyne.*
> *You must soon switch off your valves, I must soon switch*
> *off mine.*
> *Write back and say you have heard me, your " hook up "*
> *and where and how,*
> *Quick ! for the engine's failing, good-bye, you old low–*
> *brow !*